Come, Play with the Angels

A Playbook in Self Discovery and Spirit Recovery

Betty Rae Calleja

Published in the USA by
Proctor Publications
PO Box 2498, Ann Arbor, MI 48106

LCCN 96–72418

Cataloging in Publication Data
Prepared by Quality Books Inc.

Calleja, Betty Rae.
Come play with the angels : a playbook in self discovery
and spirit recovery / Betty Rae Calleja.
p. cm.
ISBN: 1–882792–39–4

1. Angels.   2. Guardian angels.   I. Title.
BT966.2.C35 1997   235′.3
                                          QBI97–40042

Dedication

To all those who have sought my help
as a clairvoyant. It is through them
that I have learned so much.

And to my husband, Joe.

Acknowledgments

To all my Angels in Spirit,
most especially my own Guardian Angels, Hagar and Omar.

To all my "Angels" in beautiful human bodies, especially:

Angel Peggy Hare, my daughter and kindred spirit,
whose unconditional love and acceptance have been my joy;

Angel Wendy Sercombe who has always
inspired me with new ideas;

Angel Pat Kauffman whose faithful encouragement,
infectious laughter and fresh insights kept me at it;

Angel Dorothy Oswald, now in spirit and truly an angel,
who never let me give up and commanded me to
"Turn on that computer!"

All the Angels in the "Halo Club"
who have given me courage and taught me so much;

Angel Hazel Proctor for her beautiful artwork
and encouragement. Angel Sarah Newland for her
patience in editing my manuscript.

And to my Angel husband, Joe, for his honest comments,
his faithful support and his enduring belief in me.

Thank you!

Table of Contents

Preface

In 1981, I began this book under the title *The Road to Joy*. It might have been better to call it *The Journey of a Timid Soul*, with fifteen years of trials and errors, of surging forward and cowardly retreating. It is a story of success, for I have proven the universal law that states, "What we focus on expands." At this point in my life, I know that illusive Imp, Joy, on a daily basis. My cup does indeed run over and flood all I meet. People often say, "You're like sunshine. I feel good when I'm with you." And they ask, "Are you always this happy? Don't you ever get depressed?" Yes, I *am* always happy because I have studied with the angels and learned their tricks of opening to the light of Joy and closing off the darkness of fear and depression.

This is the story of a seeker who persisted in knowing Joy despite many roadblocks that loomed up in her path. It was not an easy road to travel. But everyone has challenges. That's life. The most significant part of my study is that I was not always joyful like I am now. I studied it. I practiced it. I learned it. I became it and so can anyone else willing to take the journey.

My introduction to angels was given later in life. Oh, I knew *about* them, I just hadn't *met* them yet. I had to overcome my cowardice and acknowledge that visions and "knowing" were a natural experience in everyone. Some people tell me that I'm different from other psychics they have met. They say there is a more spiritual quality to my readings. Perhaps this is so because a coward runs for help. I *ask the angels to help me*. First, I go to the Commander in Chief, God, and ask permission to bring Divine knowledge and wisdom to the person seeking my help. "He/She/It" sends in the troops – angels. And they come. They bring with them the most incredible feeling of unconditional love and joy that I have ever experienced. After a reading, I am filled with enormous energy. I suspect that in my ignorance about "metaphysics" and all the "rituals" that can go with it, I am like David and Goliath. The only weapon I take into this metaphysical world is my slingshot of innocence. And the angels carry me through into Joy. This is what people feel from my readings. The privilege of sharing this special joy continuously uplifts and fills my soul to overflowing.

With the background of a trained teacher, it came naturally for me to share my discoveries with others. *Come, Play with the Angels* is the title I was inspired to give an adult education class that began in 1994. It was a six-week program of discovering answers to life's questions. I offered it after many requests from clients who wanted to know more of the teachings from my angels. We used guided imagery, dream interpretation, hands-on projects and free-flowing journal writing. My students were encouraged to discover their own angels who would inspire them with insights that would uplift and change their lives for the better.

I put together a "play-book" rather than a work-book. I've always believed we learn better if it's fun and not work. In the class, I introduced the students to an angel a week, giving a guided meditation followed by questions to aid them in beginning their journal writing. Each week, I also introduced a new idea about how to cope with life's twists and turns through deep relaxation and creative visualization. We played and laughed and learned together – both my students and myself.

The enthusiastic reception from those who became "Graduates in the Art of Playing with the Angels" spilled over into a weekly study group. It was obvious there was a great need for this kind of knowledge that was spiritual, but not "religious." It was experiential and open – not dogmatic. It explored new ideas with no pressure to accept any of it. We came up with a group purpose statement that is worth including here. "Our purpose as a group, called *The Halo Club*, is to obtain spiritual growth through intellectual stimulation, group discussion and meditation so we may reach our highest potential as spiritual, mental, physical and emotional beings in a setting of total acceptance and non-judgment." We selected various books for study and discussion, observing different viewpoints of truth. It is my purpose to help the group find their own truth.

As more and more people began to ask me for something that I had written, I realized that the angels were at it again. Each new project has been planned by my angels. They drop them on me one by one like a water balloon. I get drenched in the ideas and lose a part of my life in the effort to materialize them.

I have two guardian angels. Most people have only one. Perhaps I *need them more* for all the work they ask of me! But in the beginning, I didn't know anything about them. They knew when to hide and when to appear. They knew what a coward I was. I would have run and hidden had they appeared before I was ready. I only knew about an inner drive to find and express joy in my world, probably because my own life at that time was filled with so much pain and sadness.

There are many who say "life is the pits." At one time I might have agreed with them, but now I prefer to see life as full of wonderful challenges. Each soul with its angel carefully plan each experience to send us. They give us the opportunity to play many roles on life's stage. I'm always playing the student. I may *think* I'm a teacher after thirty plus years in public school music and Language Arts, but my students were my teachers. I may *think* I played the role of a mother and grandmother, but my children taught me more. I've been cast in various roles as sales trainer, secretary, job developer, published author, composer, artist, actress and performer. But my most favorite role has been "Angel Interpreter" to more people than I can remember. That position has had many titles. Some call me clairvoyant or visionary, others say I am a "true intuitive" and still others call me a mystic and psychic.

Angelic truth and wisdom would drop on me at the strangest times. It wasn't until I was in the midst of emotional chaos that serenity and joy awakened within my soul. Even though tears flowed often and great changes were happening in my outside world, inside I was at peace. Contrary as it seemed, I was actually joyful.

And it was while I was experiencing that "dark night of the soul," that I met my angels. Little by little they made themselves known to me until I not only knew of them but could "see" them.

This book highlights my journey into joy through learning to play with the angels.

All of the people mentioned in this book (except my husband, Joe) have been given fictitious names to protect their privacy. Although this is my own unique path, we are part of the one Source that links us all together. I draw upon my own personal experiences and those of my clients to use as examples to clarify the concepts the angels have given me. I encourage you to trust that you, too, can play with the angels and experience joy. I have learned that angels are the joy and peace that have become my constant companions. May they also be yours.

Introduction

Come, Play with the Angels is a course in the language of angels. It explores angelic attributes and leads to a rediscovery of your divine spirit. Probably the most important part of communicating with your angel is that you come to *understand your purpose for being here.* In learning to Play with the Angels, we will introduce many techniques for creating those wondrous angelic qualities that include serenity, joy, patience and abundant love.

We each have a guardian angel assigned to us. Its purpose is to assist our souls in accomplishing the greatest good possible in life. Angels seek to bring knowledge and peace into our lives – if we'll let them. But because we have free choice, we often do not listen to their gentle suggestions that would move us quickly to our goals.

An equally important reason for communicating with your angel is to learn how to keep your mind and body healthy. There is so much stress in each day that we don't even realize what a toll it takes until illness strikes. Yet, most of us almost *expect* to become ill with a cold, virus infection or at least a headache. The magazine ads and TV commercials that sell all kinds of medicinal drugs indoctrinate our minds to believe we will *need them to be well.* For most of us, our "medicine cabinets" are filled with vitamins and over-the-counter drugs, plus prescriptions as well. But there is a better and easier way to stay healthy and happy.

The angels and I stress using the playful imagination that we abandoned as a child. Christ said, "Unless you become as little children, you cannot enter the Kingdom of Heaven." And that simply means to allow yourself to let go of all negative beliefs and useless adult worries. Worry and doubt are the biggest stumbling-blocks from hearing our angels. Jesus also reminded us that the Kingdom of Heaven was *within each of us.* It is the angel's purpose to guide us ever inward into that joyous inner kingdom. There is nothing in our lives that cannot be changed for good. We only need to "tune in" to the wondrous wisdom of our angel to learn that for ourselves.

Angels appear to me as large spheres of pulsating light. Sometimes they take on an exquisite human form. They sometimes communicate with words, but mostly through images that are symbolic and at other times reflect reality. They present me with whole ideas like an aura of mist that surrounds my head. I search to find words to describe what I *know* in order to pull them into the physical world. Abstract, spiritual concepts are hard to pin down. But it is well worth it to become an "Angel Interpreter."

As you begin our course in angelic *attributes,* let your mind and heart release all preconceived ideas about angels. This book is not a treatise on angels, but rather an exploration and study of their language. In each chapter, I introduce a common question that has been asked of me during the readings I have given to hundreds of people over the years. In taking each question to the individual's guardian angel, I am given the most astounding answers. It is through these readings for others that I have learned so much. Now the angels encourage me to share this with you.

Allow yourself a week to study and play with the ideas presented in each chapter. You may read the entire book first, and then go back to one chapter at a time for in-depth study. To help you become aware of your angel, each chapter introduces you to a new way of looking at your life. The questions that follow are for you to consider as stepping-stones into your Inner Sanctum. To know one's self is to love the Self. . . the soul within. Each discovery of your true self breaks the illusions that try to keep you in the dark.

There are four "Journeys with Your Guardian Angel" on the two tapes that accompany this book. Listen to side one of the tapes for the entire first week, side two for the second week, etc. Each side begins with a relaxation exercise and then takes you through a playful visualization of your guardian angel. Each exercise enables you to slow down the babble of the conscious mind. Through these imaginary visits with your angel, you will be amazed at the insights that will come to you. Trust this and believe in yourself. Each session will make it easier and easier for you to go to your own Inner Sanctum, until you will not need the tapes anymore. If you practice the suggestions given, you should be able to listen to your own angel's loving guidance any time you slow your mind and go within.

Journal writing is the most important part of this course in learning the language of angels. Buy a journal that looks and feels good. It is important that you even select a pencil or pen that is comfortable for you. Don't worry about spelling or grammar. Use your own shorthand like "&" for and or "w/" for with. If you have a computer and can type fluently, use that instead. Whatever works.

Some people have expressed their concern about writing in a journal. They believed that if a family member read what they had written, she might be hurt or misunderstand or worse, think they were crazy. One student said she liked the idea of using a computer because she could have a password and therefore better protect her privacy. This was interesting since she lives alone. I know invasion of privacy is a real fear because I've lived through it.

My journal writing began 30 years ago. I called my journal Som, which meant "Soul of me." But you can imagine what impressions my ex-husband got when he read a conversation with Som *who answered back!* Yes, I carried on a conversation with my journal and **pretended** to receive answers. The amazing part is that *I really did!* The journal allowed me to blow off steam from hurt and anger that was building up from a dysfunctional relationship. I *imagined* how my guardian angel would respond. I knew angels were uplifting, encouraging and supportive. I knew they accepted me for who I was without criticism or condemnation. So I wrote in that manner until it was a natural way to respond. But when Todd read it, he told the children their mom was "losing it." He really became concerned that I was going crazy.

During one of our many sessions with a marriage counselor, I bravely handed her my journal and asked her to read it and give me her opinion. Two heart-pounding weeks later, she returned it saying, "I don't know where this comes from, Betty Rae, but your journal has given you more coping skills than I ever can. Your only problem is you believe you have no choice in this marriage. You do. You can choose to stay or you can choose to leave." She went on to say that I really didn't need her. "You're one of the most sane people I've ever met." We hugged, I left and never returned.

I also chose to leave that 32-year marriage. My journal revealed patterns in that relationship that were destructive and hurtful. My angels helped me overcome fears of ridicule and criticism, of loss of love and of being alone.

By using your journal to *observe life*, you can become aware of how others can "push your buttons." When you begin to see how you react, you can begin to change it. You can choose again. Unlike a diary that records the day's events, a journal records your feelings and reactions to those events. It enables you to pay attention to life from each personal encounter and release those blocks to your happiness. Fear has an insidious way of blocking our ability to see clearly. Anxieties about ridicule, condemnation, failure, or loss of money or love can be the most damaging because they stop us before we even begin. Yet fear has a way of confronting us, giving us opportunities to face and overcome them. Learning to trust, like a little child who believes in Santa, *or a guardian angel,* is extremely difficult at times. I encourage you to begin now to do so.

To keep an accurate account that will be meaningful to you a year from now, it is important that you give the date: time, day, month and year. When you answer the questions for the week's journal entries at the end of each chapter, be sure to include the question as part of your answer so that it makes sense later.

Your journal can become your best friend. Allow your heart to be open and your angels will touch you with such profound love and wisdom that you will be filled with joy.

As you read the ideas and concepts in this book, use whatever you find useful and discard the rest. The angels and I would never impose upon you any belief that is not comfortable for you. Simply let it go.

Because self-discovery can sometimes be painful, I want to stress again "playing" rather than working at the exercises in this book. In a lighthearted manner, you can more easily let go of anxieties and be ready for fun.

It would be ideal to study this course with a small group of friends who can be loving and supportive. Stress the importance of nonjudgment and total acceptance like the *Halo Club* has become for each person in it. This is such a gift. Group discussion is a tool for increased comprehension and understanding. I highly encourage it. We don't always see ourselves clearly. Illusion is a mask we all wear. The questions at the end of each chapter are good for group discussion as well as journal writing.

For you to get the most out of Playing with the Angels, it is important that you love and pamper yourself during this eight-week period. Get plenty of rest, eat lots of fruit and vegetables with very little meat. Breathe fresh air; go for walks; laugh a lot. Be sure that you balance these weeks between work, play, prayer and rest. Too much of any one thing can create confusion in the mind and discomfort in the body.

You could easily read this book in a week, put it aside and forget about it. But if you really wish to hear your own guardian angel, you will make a commitment to self discovery by following the suggestions given. This is not accomplished in a week. It took you more than a week to obtain the mindsets that created your life thus far. Know that it will take you as long as you need to change your life for the better. By signing the "Agreement with My Angel" on the following page, your angel will know that you are really serious about learning to listen. And, let me tell you from experience, it most certainly is worth hearing! Time and again, my angels have said, "Be at peace, Beloved. Rejoice and be glad in all things." To this I say, "Amen! Peace be with you."

– Betty Rae

An Agreement With My Angel

I,_____ , understand that in order
to be successful in learning to Play with the Angels, I must commit
myself to take the time needed to explore the ideas and activities
presented. I agree to read one chapter a week and write my observations, thoughts and feelings each day as my angel presents them
to me.

I,_____ , further realize that this
experience may raise feelings and questions for me to resolve. Since
this may require great energy from me, I hereby determine with
unwavering firmness to take wondrous care of myself through exercise, good food, relaxation and rest. I agree to gently and lov-
ingly pamper myself for this period of time.

_____ Signature

_____ Date

Chapter 1
What Are Angels?

Dear Guardian Angel,
I see you're made of flesh like me.
Your pictures say it's so.
Yet, your wings are like a bird who sings.
Which is which? I want to know.

When I see you standing by my bed,
Your light shines like a candle's glow.
You're not at all like your pictures say.
Why is that? I want to know.
– A Curious Soul

Angels In Art and Literature

What are angels? Are there really "light" and "dark" angels? How are they alike? How are they different? As you read these questions, your own answers have formed within your mind. Each person pulls out the stops on their deeply held beliefs from early religious training. The stories stick like glue. And writers such as Edgar Allen Poe, John Milton and Steven King will capitalize upon those beliefs to give us a few thrills.

Ever since I began teaching a class in angelic "attributes," people have presented me with dozens of books on the subject as well as representations of these wondrous beings in all shapes and forms from hanging crystal angels to crocheted angels. The more I read, the more confused I became about who and what angels really are. One source briefly described each rank of Angels, giving its choir, purpose and names. For example, the Seraphim are in the First Hierarchy – First Choir. They are considered Spirits of Love who are immediately next to God. They are said to provide the universe with the positive spirit of fiery love. They have been given the color of red or crimson. They are given the names of Michael, Seraphiel, Jehoel, Metatron, Kemuel, Uriel and Nathanael.

They say there are seven different choirs of angels: Seraphim, Cherubim, Thrones, Dominions, Virtues, Powers, Princes, Archangels and Angels. It's interesting that there were no names given for that last group of Third Hierarchy – Third Choir as though these lowest of angels weren't very important. All of this information made my mind spin. Does this mean that there are seven different choral groups with different choral directors? Do they have to audition for each group or are they promoted to it? What if they can't sing? Or worse yet, what if they hate to sing? I've had some students in my choirs who were sent there by counselors to get them out of other teachers' hair.

Many ancient myths and beliefs have also influenced the many creative expressions of angels. Artists Paul Rubens and Anthony Van Dyck loved to show naked babies as chubby little Cherubs in their religious paintings. Today, they'd probably be jailed for child pornography! But Cherubs are the plural form for Cherubim, which is the second highest rank in the angel hierarchy – no babies there! In the Christian Bible, Cherubim are portrayed as welding flaming swords while guarding the Tree of Life. On the other hand, the Greek god, Cupid, was always portrayed as a baby with a bow and arrow aiming a heart at some unsuspecting victim. The Greeks called him Eros, which is symbolic of *sensuous love*. Mix and match and add confusion!

If those Cherubim with the flaming swords guarded the Tree of Life in the garden of Eden, where were they when Eve wandered into the garden – on coffee break? And how did the Snake get by them? Come to think of it, no one was guarding the Tree of Knowledge of Good and Evil from which that first lady picked the apple. So how come God didn't put angels to protect it and save all of us this trouble? Was it perhaps the "Divine Plan" that each of us *experience good and evil* as part of our spiritual education?

Most of our understanding of angels comes from writings of ancient scriptures such as the Christian Bible, the Kabbalah, The

Lost Sea Scrolls, the writings of teachers like Aristotle or St. Thomas Aquinas, legend and myth, or from fiction writers such as John Milton in *Paradise Lost*. In all of these manuscripts, the Bible's influence on us about angels is probably referred to the most. It also makes us quite aware of demons as the opposing force against which the angels do battle.

Many of the 14th century artists portrayed the battle between good and evil with the good guys looking like strong, beautiful men with feathered wings while the bad guys were ugly and wore bat's wings or looked like dragons. Perhaps those myths of Merlin and the dragons crept into our religious beliefs, or maybe the artists draw upon them to portray the vivid words of the Bible? I'm sure writings like Dante's *Inferno* and Milton's *Paradise Lost* have probably inspired more artists to create their battles of good and evil through angels and demons. Milton's classic bedazzled the minds of millions over the years with his profound story of human endeavor to overcome obstacles. According to him, Satan had rebelled at being instructed to bow down to Christ and, in resistance, he gathered round him a third of all the angels of heaven.

"Wide was spread
That war, and various: sometimes on firm ground
A standing fight; then, soaring on main wing,
Tormented all the air; all air seemed then
Conflicting fire.
A wondrous thing it was to see his head,
Wearing three faces, scarlet to the fore;. . .
Beneath each head two mighty wings emerged. . .
No feathers did they bear but like a bat's
There covering was." (Book 6, *Paradise Lost*)

With rhetoric like that, is it any wonder people are frightened at the thought of demons? What powerful adversaries they were portrayed to be. Who'd want to mess with them! I had to laugh at my eldest brother who calls himself an "agnostic." Awhile back he read the book, *The Exorcist* and said that it was enough to scare him into believing in God. Perhaps *that's* the purpose of demons!

Paintings of angels over the centuries are numbered in the thousands. Since a picture is worth a thousand words, is it any wonder people have been impressed with the concept of good and evil? And is it not possible that there can be a great deal of misinformation about angels as well? But in this century, on the verge of great changes in the physical world and in spirit, angels are working very hard to bring out the truth about themselves and God, their Creator.

As I continued to pour over the library of literature on angels, I began to understand that each religion and race has their own special angels. One dictionary of angels *and demons* had 362 pages with a bibliography of over 1,000 references. I was impressed! Reading it was even more impressive – and confusing. It seems that each angel named had several different versions of who and what it is or represents. Every religion has its share of angelic lore and tells the story differently. Take Michael as an example. You'd think he would be quite simple, such a powerful angel. Well, he's not. Some sources said Michael is as God and ranks as the greatest of all angels, whether in Jewish, Christian, or Islamic writings, secular or religious. He originates from the Chaldean tradition where he was considered almost a god. He wears many hats from being in charge of the order of virtues and the archangels, to being the angel of repentance. The information goes on and on giving Michael different names like Midrash Rabba in Exodus 18 as well as being credited as the essence in the fire that Moses saw in the burning bush. The more I read, the more overwhelmed I became. It seemed to me that every writer who turned to pen and paper had a different story to tell about angels. Now we are reading about angels who are teaching us about love, kindness and beauty.

In *Angel Answers: A Joyful Guide to Creating Heaven on Earth*, (Pocket Books, 1995), Andrew Ramer writes, "For thousands of years you have learned from suffering and pain. Now you are ready to learn from love and joy instead. Now is the time when all of humanity can come together to create Heaven on Earth. Everyone who is alive now is a part of the transformation. Everyone who is alive now is needed in the transformation. Every moment is another opportunity to awaken."

It seems that Ramer says all I wanted to say. And with the hundreds of books out there, why does anyone need *my* book, I asked my angels, Hagar and Omar. They smiled and patiently said, "They do." I couldn't get off the hook. My own doubts and fears often crowded out my light of joy – for a moment or two. Like when I discovered the names of these angels. Oh, I had to ask! When they told me, "Hagar and Omar," I dropped them like hot flames of hell. Who ever heard of angel names like that? It took two weeks before I had enough courage to finally ask them. They said *I had given them those names when I could see them in an Arabian incarnation.* I said, "Oh. Can I change them now?" They answered, "Yes, if you choose to. Our names are a vibration or sound and difficult to translate into physical language. But we will answer to whichever name you choose."

Well, after they had explained it so nicely, I figured I'd keep their names. I have simply accepted them because over the years they have proven themselves through their unconditional love and wisdom. I am most grateful that they have made themselves known to me in this lifetime. They are the ones who give me all the information I receive in each reading. They have never failed me, even when I believed I would fail. Curiously, I did not "read up on angels" once I became aware of them. I had no desire to "study" angels. I accepted them as a fact of life.

Belief in "Good" and "Evil"

You've heard people say they have an angel on one shoulder and the devil on the other. They are relating to the pull between positive and negative energy that is found only in the physical dimension. Many religions are steeped in the fear of "Evil" and "Satan" and "Demons." Fear is a mighty powerful source of energy. There are those who worship the Devil, drawing power from that negative polarity.

But the problem with negative energy is that it is destructive like a boomerang. "If you live by the sword, you'll die by the sword." "You will reap what you sow." These sayings define the law of cause and effect that is working all the time, even if we are unaware of it. If we dabble in negative energy with the idea of manipulating others for our own gain without concern for the good of all, we're in trouble. Whatever harm we cause another, we will experience it in like form sometime, somewhere, if not in this life-time then in another. Even if you don't believe that, the possibility of it is enough to make you think twice, isn't it?

Good and evil are part and parcel of this physical world. I like to think some souls come to this giant amusement park to take the scariest rides they can find. When the personality of the soul for-gets who it really is – spirit – fear of the unknown becomes the greatest fear of all. Demons do that for us. They represent the nega-tive polarity of this planet. They are the antagonists in our drama while our souls take the role of leading character or protagonist. Or you could say that the angels are the heroes with the demons playing the villains in a world just another dimension away, like spiritual star wars.

As my imagination takes flight with all the books on angels, it makes me wonder what is truth. It was people who wrote about them in every sacred scripture. And people who told stories about those stories and drew pictures about the stories. It is people who described what they believed they saw from a background of fear-filled beliefs. Belief in good and evil creates the world in which we live, for our thoughts attract like a magnet.

On a television show about haunted houses, an intuitive was interviewed about her work with "ghosts." Her success at "clean-ing house" was impressive. And the most important thing she said was, "Don't be afraid of them. They feed on fear. It gives them energy. Instead, love them; bless them; talk to them, and release them into the Light." My soul sang with the truth of this.

Over and over my angels have said, "Be at peace." "Be not afraid." They show how each event or experience in my life can be good. No matter what pain or grief I've experienced, they have turned it into a gem of hidden wisdom. Even through an experi-ence with "Evil."

My friend, Mary, asked me to come to her place of work and give a reading to her friend, Judy. I was still new at giving readings and was not aware of the power or the effect other people's minds and beliefs could have on me. Yes, I had heard about "protecting myself," by imagining myself in "white light." I don't remember if I did it at this particular time.

My angels had shown me a dream about using an amethyst crystal to enhance my readings. They gave me the tool that opened my mind to "past life" readings that have become so helpful to people. At this time, I was just beginning to experiment with my crystal for readings and brought it with me. Judy was managing the adult day-care that Mary owned.

I began the reading by taking the crystal from Judy that she had held for a few minutes while we chatted. I took my slow deep breaths and settled myself. I began to see confusion and fear surrounding this lady. I saw that she had been abused as a child and almost wept for her. Her need for love was tremendous. Then I saw a powerful entity standing beside her who looked like an Indian Chief. Judy said it was "Red Feather." I remembered having seen him in a previous reading that I had done for her, telling her of the love that this guide had for her. But now, something was different. There was a fierce protection, or was it control that I felt coming from this entity? I tried to speak with it, but it avoided me.

Suddenly I felt myself being pulled into an energy vortex, like a whirlpool that swept me into a black hole. Mary says that I began moaning and rocking back and forth. I didn't respond to her questions. She became alarmed and grabbed the crystal out of my hands. It brought me right out of it. We all sat in silence staring at one another. "What happened?" I asked. Mary and Judy shook their heads, having no answers to give.

What happened I learned later was that Judy was a multiple personality whose great need for love had turned the idea of a loving guide into a possessive lover. Her fear, anger and self-hatred had turned her guide into an evil thought form that possessed her every waking moment, raping her and physically abusing her. The mind is very powerful. We often underestimate it. We can create reality as often through fear as through love. What I had experienced was her own negative energy projecting itself against me from seeing what was really happening. If I had, it would have ended her fantasies that she so desperately clung to. In my naivete, I walked right into something for which I was totally unprepared. But after this experience, I encouraged Judy to get professional help, which she did.

I saw this lovely lady a couple of years later. She was almost well. I sensed the change immediately. The doctor had discovered six different personalities, and she had integrated all but two. She also said that she knew why I went through my experience with her. Judy told of the devil worship her parents had forced her to participate in and sexual abuse they put her through. It was obvious all of this fear, negativity and hatred had wounded her soul.

You'd think an experience like that would have made me hang up my crystal forever! When I went to Hagar and asked what had happened to me, he explained that I didn't need to fear the negative force in another individual or anywhere. I was Divinely guided and protected. Hagar reminded me that I had asked for Mary to remain during the reading – something I didn't ordinarily do. Both of my angels were prepared to step in. They knew this was an experience I had needed to help me become more aware of the power of negative energy. I was also reassured that the power of Love was greater. Because I was still skeptical and new at giving readings, I did have fear surrounding it. That fear became an energy that overwhelmed me and froze me within it. I have also found that people who are manic-depressive are very hard to read because their electromagnetic field is scattered and very erratic.

On another occasion – and there have been only two – I was visiting some friends of Joe's at their magnificent $500,000 new home. Rob and Alicia were delighted to show it off to me. Like Joe and I, they, too, were newlyweds. As the afternoon and evening wore on I noticed a drain of energy within me. I felt a headache coming on and was becoming increasingly tired. I yearned to go home. We finally left and arrived home about midnight. I became violently ill, vomiting until I had dry heaves. I was puzzled about the event. No, I hadn't had anything to drink – I'm a teetotaler. And no, it wasn't anything I had had to eat. Everyone else was fine.

Finally, I went to my mentor and friend, Ann, and asked her what had happened. She "saw" that Alicia was in the midst of family turmoil. Having married a rich man, his children were envious and fearful that their "inheritance" would be squandered by this interloper. I was amazed at her insight. Alicia had been relating the horrid details to me all day. Ann said, "You have been absorbing all the negative energy that fills that home. Did you surround yourself in Light before you went?" she asked.

"Of course not," I recounted. "Why should I have?"

"Because of what you've experienced, that's why!"

"You mean that violent illness was caused by my visit to friends?!" I was astounded.

Ann chuckled, "I'll bet your friends feel a whole lot better today than you do – for many reasons. First, you cleansed their home by taking away their negativity. And second, your love and concern lifted their souls out of fear. I'll bet you gave them some sound advice, if I know you at all."

"Well, I did have a few suggestions," I chuckled. Alicia seemed to agree and said she would act upon them. One simple suggestion was to create a will that would ensure Rob's children that they would not be left out, but to also ensure Alicia that she would be taken care of should Rob pass away.

"You could have avoided all that, you know," Ann reprimanded gently.

"Yeah, I guess so," I replied. I must have sounded unsure because Ann had more to say.

"The minute you began to notice a drain in your energy, you should have gone within and replenished it as well as mentally surrounded yourself in Divine Light. That boost of positive energy would have carried you through the experience without any repercussions." I was truly grateful for her knowledge and wisdom.

After my scary ride with the lady with multiple personalities, you had better believe that I have respect for the negative pull of life. I learned a lot from that encounter with "evil." It forced me to examine old beliefs that let me buy into that fear drama. Unfortunately, (or fortunately), I have little firsthand knowledge about this "force of evil" with which to draw any conclusions. But, you see, I can't really accept "evil" as having any power over me unless I and my soul *choose* to experience it, otherwise my angels simply wouldn't allow it.

Personal Encounters with Angels

You can read all about angels but personal encounters are the best. Guardian angels show themselves to me as a bright light pulsating and swirling in a pattern of energy that looks something like champagne bubbles flowing up and down and around a shape like a human form. Angels have told me that they do not have "wings." Their energy swirls and pulsates in such a way that visionaries and mystics of the past may have mistaken the flow of energy to look like wings. They certainly don't need them because they can be anywhere in less than the wink of an eye.

Long ago, Hagar explained that he was a pure spirit assisting me through this adventure into the physical. He tells me that angels are of a very high frequency vibration that not only makes them invisible, but of a higher realm than individual personalities who have gone beyond the Earth's dimension. Because vibration is sound, they really do not have names as we know them. Rather, their names are more like music. But they have cooperated with our needs and supplied names – or as in my case, allowed us to give them names. They will faithfully come to whatever we call them – even when we don't call at all! Guardian angels are assigned to each soul who enters the physical state. Everyone has one and more people are becoming aware of it.

Hope Price writes accounts of people who have met what they believed to be angels. *In Angels: True Stories of How They Touch Our Lives*, (Avon Books, 1993), she includes a story by Captain Cecil Wightwick Hayward, Staff Officer in the 15th Corps Intelligence, British Army Headquarters. He says, "While a detachment of British soldiers was retiring through Mons under very heavy gunfire, they knelt behind a hastily erected barricade and endeavored to hold up the enemy advance. The firing on both sides was very intensive and the air reverberated with deafening crashes of exploding shells. Suddenly, firing on both sides stopped dead and a silence fell. Looking over their barriers, the astonished British saw four or five wonderful beings much bigger than men between themselves and the Germans. They were white-robed and bare-headed, and seemed rather to float than stand. Their backs were toward the British, and they faced the Germans with outstretched arms and hands. The sun was shining quite brightly at the time. Next thing the British knew was the Germans were retreating in great disorder."

Karen Goldman has collected many stories of how angels help people in her book, *Angel Encounters* (Simon & Schuster, 1995). One little eight-year old boy describes seeing a "mean little spirit. . .It wasn't scary, but it was mean. . ." When he called his grandmother to come, she told him God would chase them away. "So I went back to my room and all I saw were three little angels. The mean little spirits, they just left." He exclaimed that he liked angels and felt safe when they were around."

Another very precocious little boy of about five or six wrote about his experiences with angels and spirits way back in 1885. It wasn't his Victorian parents that suggested this, but his private tutor who saw the gift of "second sight" as it was called then. *The Boy Who Saw True* (C.W. Daniel Co. Limited, 1986), is a delightful account of a child's eye view of spirits whom he saw as easily as anyone in the physical. He was also aware of the "lights" around people that changed as their moods changed and revealed the truth about themselves, even if they tried to hide it.

Angels Bring Light

GUARDIAN ANGELS ARE:
Beings of Light – Pure Spirits from God;
Cheerleaders and Playmates
who uplift and inspire;

Instruments of Change
who bring people and events together;
Guardians and Protectors
who save us from ourselves;
God's Messengers
who bring good news and glad Tidings!

The angels bring us many aspects of "seeing true." Long ago, I suspect we all saw the "lights" or auras that surround every living creature. Early painters drew halos of light around religious figures. Eastern religions call these lights "chakras" or energy centers that encircle the physical body. The Chinese have known about these energy centers for ages in their practice of acupuncture. A special kind of photography can even show the colors of these "lights" that change with our emotional climate. There are more and more people today, who with their ability to see auras, have been able to help heal the physical body.

Each week in my class, "Come, Play with the Angels," I introduced a new attribute of an angel. One I called the "Angel of Light." The dictionary has many definitions for the word "light," including a few interpretations pertaining to our needs: "Noun: 1. Electromagnetic radiation that can be perceived by the human eye; 2. The sensation or perception of such radiation – brightness; 3. The illumination, such as the sun or an electric lamp, [or an angel!]; 4. A way of looking at or considering something; 5. Understanding – enlightenment. Verb: To be revealed; to see the light; to perceive a hitherto hidden meaning."

I am called by some a "clairvoyant" which means one who sees clearly. It means perceiving things that are out of the range of human senses. I tell my clients that when they begin to open their minds, using their imagination, their angels will amaze them with new understanding and knowledge. They will begin to have greater insights into everyday events and experiences. I do not understand how I see another person's life, describing in detail their family, their successes and sorrows. I just know that I do. I do not believe that I am unique in this. I would not be writing this book if I did. I believe that you can gain knowledge from your angel as well.

I have been told that my "Divine Mission" is to help people remember who they really are – spirits – and to bring them that inner peace and joy that is their natural state of being. I am not alone in this mission. I believe that each of us are given insights that allow us to be of service to one another.

I believe that the angels are here in force to direct more and more Divine Light upon this dark and weary planet. And that Light is becoming more visible in people like Terry Lynn Taylor who has a light-hearted sweetness about her writings in *Messenger of Light* (J.H. Kramer, Inc., 1990). It's another example of the many people who are having direct contact with angels. "**Light**-heart training teaches you to attract angels by becoming angelic. Think of **light**-heart training as a process of growing feathers! Being angelic is a sure way to attract angels (birds of a feather flock together). As we know, angels take themselves **light**ly, but what can this do for us? Simply put, developing a **light** heart brings out our natural ability to be entertaining, charming, and clever, and allows us to rediscover our innate sweetness."

Spirit Guides and Angels

When I hear people talk about a grandmother as being their guardian angel, I shake my head and explain the facts as I know them. That's not to say that a grandmother can't act like a guardian angel to you. Love is the motivating factor. But just because someone is in spirit, doesn't make them all-knowing and all-wise. Not even the angels are that. Only God is. Whenever we hear about the "wisdom" from someone's spirit guide, become wary. Some spirits, as I have found, love to expound on every subject you can think about. When they find someone to listen, they never want to shut up.

On the other hand, some people have been given a spirit guide in addition to their guardian angel to help them with a life-task. Rosemary Altea resisted the idea of a "guide" for quite some time, but reluctantly accepted "Grey Eagle" as her partner in her work of bringing loved ones together – from the spirit world. Altea tells of her remarkable work with the deceased in her book, *The Eagle and the Rose*, (Warner Books, Inc., 1995). Grey Eagle is a spirit from an American Indian lifetime and counsels Rosemary when she gets stuck with a timid or stubborn spirit.

Others have been able to be a channel through which a spirit entity can speak. Pat Rodegast and Judith Stanton have brought us the beautiful and simple thoughts of an entity called Emmanuel who, although not an angel, has a great deal of wisdom. For example, he says, "You all sit in a shower of Light, wondering why it is dark. It is your minds that rummage around in the vast dictionaries of history to research the word 'Light.' The fundamental purpose of life is not just to be comfortable or to feel safe. Passage into seeming darkness involves pain, suffering, chaos. Having duly arrived in the darkness, it does seem that many are content to remain there. That is because they are too frightened to move. They believe that if they hold their breath and endure, it will go away. In every soul's journey there must be a moment when the question is raised: 'What is this all about?' It is at that precise moment that the light is available. In this way suffering serves a noble purpose."

We are Light Beings living in a dark world. It seems that all around us is misery, poverty, starvation, brutality, incest, rape, murder and on and on. Newspapers and television blast our senses with it constantly. How can our lights shine with all that? By becoming aware of our guardian angel and beginning to listen to the wisdom that comes from them. They tell us to giggle and laugh, to see the larger picture as they do. They urge us to turn off the TV and see life from an angelic viewpoint, beholding both heaven and Earth. The Bible speaks of the "veil" that blinds us from seeing God and Its angels. That veil is the darkness of our own fears. Once we enter into a joyous attitude, the veil is lifted and we see "heaven."

You can see the angel's handiwork as more people are recording their glimpses of heaven through near-death experiences. Betty Eadie wrote of her adventure in *Embraced By The Light* (Gold Leaf Press, 1992), describing in detail the beauty of heaven. "I saw a pinpoint of light in the distance. . .as I approached it, I noticed the figure of a man standing in it, with the light radiating all around him. As I got closer the light became brilliant. . .a golden halo. . .[that] burst out from around him and spread into a brilliant magnificent whiteness that extended out for some distance. I felt his light blending into mine. It was the most unconditional love I have ever felt, and as I saw his arms open to receive me I went to him and received his complete embrace and said over and over, 'I'm home. I'm home. I'm finally home.'"

Although the accounts of near-death adventures like Eadie may differ slightly, most tell of a Light Being that greets them on the other side. Some call it God, some say it is Jesus and others say it's their angel. Just as in ancient times, visions are interpreted according to the individual's belief-system and life experiences.

My experience with those who pass on has taught me a great deal about the after life. For awhile, a spirit called Thomas brought gentleness and wisdom to others through me. My own curiosity would not allow anyone, even an angel, to completely take over my body, yet I experienced a sort of scooting over within my mind to allow Thomas to express himself with my voice. Although I was not always aware of the words he said, I was completely aware of the concepts. I was given a visual view that remained even after Thomas left. In that way, I was able to answer questions from my client. But I was never completely comfortable with this arrangement. Although Thomas was accurate in many ways, he wasn't quite as knowledgeable as Hagar and Omar. My own angels could see quite easily into the past or the future, while Thomas seemed to resist giving that information. It was some time before I realized that Hagar gives me words, while Omar gives me pictures and creative ideas. They really make a great team.

But since my focus is on the soul and its angel, those who pass into spirit take second place unless someone asks. Even then it seems that their angel will often explain why they left, especially if it was by an accidental death, or more tragically a suicide. For example, one lady came for a reading to learn about her son who had died in a car accident. He was only 17 and it seemed to be such a waste of life. The lady's angel brought her son to me who expressed regret for causing his family such grief. Then he explained how he had committed suicide in a previous life and realized now how precious life was and that one must learn to appreciate the gift of life. The angel explained that souls who abort life will have to face their problems all over again in a future lifetime. The angel went on to explain that experience in the physical is always a balancing act. This boy was given exactly 17 years because that was how many more years *he would have lived* in the previous life. For some, this may seem harsh and unforgiving, but it is not. We do indeed *reap what we sow*. Even pain and suffering serve a purpose.

> *Angels are Mood Lifters*
> *When You Learn Their Bag Of Tricks:*
> Smile; Laugh; Giggle;
> Watch a Funny Movie; Read a Funny Book;
> Go for a Walk and Observe the Beauty of Nature;
> Hug a Tree; Plant a Flower; Buy a Bouquet;
> Light a Candle; Clean a Drawer; Visit an "Up" Friend;
> Help Someone; Create Something;
> *Refuse to Dwell on Negative Thoughts!*

Summary

Each one of us is like a diamond that radiates light from many dimensional facets or points, yet it is one diamond – God. We are all reflecting the light of God. It may be that some are more polished than others, but we're working on it.

Angels are here to uplift, inspire and increase our ability to open up to that Light of God within each of us. They are constantly urging, (but never demanding), us to look for the good in others and the world around us. They are constantly whispering suggestions in our ears to pull us out of darkness into the Light of Joy.

Each day, I have to trust that my angels know more than I. The Psalms speak often of trust. "My God in You I place my trust." (Ps. 7) The angels sing in unison with those who praise and glorify

God. How often Hagar has said, "Rejoice, Beloved! Lift up your voice in praise and thanksgiving!" And my spirit soars into Joy.

"So where does all this knowledge of angels get me?" you say. "I still don't know how to listen and hear them, even if I do believe in them." I hear you. Now we get down to work with practical suggestions on how to hear those angels. First, you will begin the journey inward to discover who you really are. There are many questions that the angels will present to you on this silent path. You will search your mind, heart and soul for the answers.

Journal Entries for Week One

Directions: Listen to Tape One all this week. Keep your journal near the place you will go to be alone, (the bathroom cabinet if necessary!). Take one or two of the questions below each day and answer them quickly and honestly without letting the mind dwell on them too long. Be spontaneous, brief and playful.

1. Describe your "Inner Sanctum." New ideas may come to you each time you listen to the tape. Remember, this is your special place within. You may add or change it as you wish.
2. Describe the flowers, the small animal, the large animal, the conversations, the river. Describe your guardian angel, its facial features, garment, feet. Does it have wings? Describe the cup and your impressions with it.
3. Write your beliefs about angels.
4. Imagine what your angel looks like; describe in detail.
5. What are your beliefs about evil? What about "dark angels?"
6. What are your beliefs about God?
7. Which of the above beliefs were given to you by your parents?
8. Examine your beliefs about the religion your parents followed.
9. Which religious beliefs do you follow now?
10. Examine your beliefs about heaven, hell and life after death.
11. Examine your beliefs about "error" and "sin."
12. Examine your beliefs about the concept of "what goes around, comes around."

Chapter 2
Who Am I?

___

Dear Soul,
You search high and low to find yourself. Look within.
You are the Spirit of God that breathed you into existence.
You are a Mind wrapped in a coat of flesh to discover all things.
You are a Body reflecting Divine Light within your DNA,
creating yourself anew each day.
You are Emotions that cast themselves into a sea of opposites.
You are Joy. And I am with you throughout it all.
–Your Guardian Angel

People can get bogged down with the cares and worries of this physical existence and forget who they really are. You are one with God who created a spark of Itself into a spirit that chose to enter the physical experience and take on a soul that created a physical body with mind and intelligence, emotions and feelings.

You cannot separate the four aspects of yourself. They should work together, but are not always aware of one another. Most forget they have a soul. They remember only that they are a personality with a name and certain characteristics. They hardly ever think about their emotions and feelings until they're hurt or abused. Some neglect their bodies until they scream in hunger or pain. But to really know who you are, you must become aware of each of the four aspects of yourself and understand how they are intertwined.

Human Beings Are:
Spirit/Soul
Mind/Intelligence
Emotions/Feelings
Physical Body created for action

First: You Are Spirit

So, what does that mean? you ask. Some people call the spirit their Higher Self. Others have named it their super-consciousness or superego. Others still call it God. It doesn't matter what you name it, just become aware that it is not a separate entity from yourself, but a part of the total you. How do you do that? By starting the process of integration. Go to that "Kingdom of God" that Christ spoke of two thousand years ago. He told his followers to be born again and to become as little children. He confounded those who were so caught up in the physical that they had forgotten who they were. He explained how that kingdom was *within you*. It's like the angels had played a little joke on everyone by hiding God right within each of you. You come here, choosing to forget who you really are, and play hide-and-seek with God. When you finally find Him in your Inner Sanctuary, you can yell, "Allie, Allie, Home Free!"

While souls are eternal and one with God, they may choose to enter the cycle of the physical. It is in this cycle of incarnations that the soul experiences the illusion of separation from God. It is this belief of isolation that grieves the soul the most. In the spirit world, which is the soul's real home, it knows peace, joy, companionship and unconditional love. When the soul takes on a body and visits this planet called Earth, it leaves that home to experience time and space and encounter many adventures. Each soul comes with great expectations of creating good that often get lost in the pull of negativity. Good intentions become blocked by the fears that are characteristic of this physical world.

James Redfield reveals this hidden Self through his bestselling book, *The Celestine Prophecy*, (Warner Books, 1993). He sends his characters on great adventures to discover what is within them – that they exist on two dimensions at once. Redfield's main character searches for ancient Peruvian manuscripts called "The Ten Insights." As we discover each lost scroll, excitement begins to build within as we recognize bits and pieces of ourselves. For example, we are shown that there is no such thing as "coincidence." When it seems to happen, we are to pay attention, for there is much more for us to learn.

How do I find my own precious Insights? How do I begin to discover my own Inner Sanctuary? How well I remember these questions when I joined a group of people who prayed for world peace. They "went into meditation." They closed their eyes, got very quiet and stayed that way for over half an hour. When they "came out," they would tell of wonderful visions and images they had "seen." I was envious. . .and confused.

When I asked how they did that, one said, "Go within."

I asked, "Where? How?"

They tried to explain, "Let go of the Ego and let your Higher Self speak."

I was lost. "My 'Ego?' What was that?" I asked. "What's my 'Higher Self?'"

They said I had to eliminate my personality and allow my spirit self to take over.

"How do I know the difference?" I wondered.

They talked about visualization – I had a great imagination, but was still lost. Little by little, I began to understand their terminology. The "Ego" represented the personality your soul assumed when it adorned a body. The "Higher Self" was another name for my soul. Apparently, they believed there was a war going on between the two. The personality was zeroed in on self-preservation which meant enjoying the thrills of the body and its comforts and living a l-o-n-g life, while the soul was interested in the "lessons" to be learned from each experience.

My guardian angels, Hagar and Omar, set me straight about all this. First of all, they did admit that the soul sometimes has trouble letting the personality know its purpose when the mind and emotions get caught up in the fear of living. But generally they get along quite well. Secondly, my angels did not like the term "lessons." They felt that this terminology creates the fear of failure, of missing something and having to do it "all over again." They would rather people think of the soul as seeking experiences that will add knowledge and wisdom to its portfolio of the physical. Actually, there were no mistakes that couldn't be used to gain wisdom. So that eliminates another fear. Some people get so anxious about making the wrong decision that they freeze in the moment, making a decision to do nothing. If anything makes a soul frustrated, that does. It cries, "Do *something!* Let's experience life's adventures for the joy of it!" This feeling is expressed in the Bible in Revelations where John has many "Insights" like, "I know you well – you are neither hot nor cold: I wish you were one or the other! But since you are merely lukewarm, I will vomit you out of my mouth!"(Rev: 3:15) That says it quite well, don't you think? If you believe that no mistake can harm you and choose to do *something* out of joy, rather than *nothing* out of fear, you can accomplish anything your soul desires.

You're probably thinking, "If I had angels like Hagar and Omar, I wouldn't have trouble making decisions either. I'd ask them." Wrong. They don't cooperate like that. I have to do my own homework and figure things out for myself like everyone else. Little by little, I studied every book on meditation that "fell in my hands." Little by little, I began to understand. Through all the ideas, contradictions and confusion, I determined that I would simplify all the terminology and help people find their Inner Sanctum a whole lot easier than what I had gone through. But I will start at the beginning, assuming nothing. And so next we will examine how the mind functions.

Second: You Are Mind

The mind is a wonderful instrument. The scientific community considers it the "Last Frontier." Research has been ongoing for centuries. From the angelic viewpoint, the mind is the receiver for images and ideas from the soul and the spirit world. It behaves very much like a radio receiver of electronic impulses, but in a more refined way. Every thought you think is sent out like a laser beam searching for the proper frequencies to become a material manifestation.

I compare the physical brain to a computer with the mind and intelligence as the software programmed by the soul. The soul brings to the body the experiences of many lives and it is from these experiences that you act and react to life. This is why some people seem so wise while others may seem so foolish. This is why some people have great talent in music at an early age while others have strange phobias. Yet, the soul and its angel must decide which talents they will nourish and develop in each lifetime. Some souls may balance the experience of great intelligence with a rest period in a mind of a retarded person. Through this, the soul can gain understanding through humility and learn about unconditional love. There is always a specific purpose for all body types and minds.

The brain is an incredible creation. It makes you appreciate the Mind of God. It coordinates every function in the body through

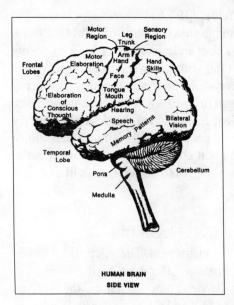

**HUMAN BRAIN
SIDE VIEW**

the telephone lines of the nervous system. These electrical signals come from the sense organs like the skin, tongue, nose, eyes and ears. People who have had brain damage have been able to reconnect or reroute these electrical circuits of the brain to regain motor, memory or verbal abilities once again.

Imagine how intricate the brain is. Each place has its own job to do. Every nerve impulse is like a telephone line that sends and receives messages through the brain. The mind never turns off even when you sleep. It stores all information, experiences and emotions. The mind draws from past experiences – even from past lifetimes – to evaluate and judge new experiences as "good" or "bad." When you go to sleep, the mind and body go on automatic pilot. The brain slows more and more, moving from the conscious state into deeper and deeper states of sleep. The brain moves in 90-minute cycles from wakefulness to deep sleep and back to the near-conscious state. All kinds of things happen during this cycle as shown in the following:

Brain Waves	Cycles/Second	Senses
Beta: Conscious Mind	15–21 Cycles	Sight, Sound, Smell, Taste, Touch, Time-Space Awareness
Alpha: Dream State	7–14 Cycles	Psychic, Intuitive, Daydreams, Visions, Dreams
Theta: Sleep State	4 – 7 Cycles	Deep Trance State, Channeling, Astral Travel
Delta: Unconscious	4 Cycles	Unknown

When you are at the **Beta** or conscious-mind brain wave level, you are aware of your physical surroundings through your five senses. You perceive everything through your belief in time-space orientation. Your perception of life is very limited with this viewpoint. You can only see one fraction of the life one moment at a time. You can only hear and smell what is around you. You can only touch that which is near. You can only taste what you put in your mouth.

When you're at the **Alpha** brain wave level, you're beyond the time-space confinement and can move into your "sixth-sense" of inner perceptions. You can visualize a lemon and your taste buds pucker. You can intuit someone nearby without seeing them. You can do so much more intuitively than most people could even imagine at this brain wave level – the level you reach when you go into light meditation. It is at the lower Alpha level that you receive visions. It is in this sleep state that you have dreams. When you slow down the conscious mind through relaxation and meditation, you allow your angel to speak with you. By slowing the brain's cycles per second, you eliminate the static of your conscious mind that interferes with higher realm communication.

The **Theta** brain wave level is an even deeper meditative state called trance. It is where you can project your spirit body and travel anywhere. And it is deep sleep. These states will be covered later in Chapter Four.

Since there is so little known scientifically about the **Delta** brain wave level, we will allow the angels to fill our imagination with "what if's." What if at this deep level of sleep, you leave your body and go visit with your angel? I'd like to believe that. Then they send you back with coded images of that private conversation. Your waking personality then plays charades with your angel, taking pictures and creating words that will make sense. This is called "dream interpretation." More on that in Chapter Six.

We introduced you to the Alpha level last week in tape one side one where you created your Inner Sanctum. Through deep relaxation and visualization, you will begin to understand that by integrating four parts of yourself, you can create inner peace and love. After you have practiced relaxation and visualization enough, you will find that you can reach the Alpha brain level with very little effort. It is then that you will realize you are hearing your angel daily.

My first attempts at meditation were a total failure. I always thought of myself as being fairly intelligent. I believed I had a "good mind." But when I tried to meditate, I felt like I just couldn't get it. My prayer group was telling me to "just go within." I was mystified as to how to do that and began searching for an answer to my dilemma. I attended a Transcendental Meditation introductory class. When they told me their course would teach me to "go within" I was gleeful. I asked, "What do I do when I get there?" They said, "Just be quiet. You don't *do* anything." My soul sent up alarm bells and I scooted out of there. If it wasn't going to help me find answers, I wanted no part of it.

Next, I went to the Silva Method of Mind Control. They explained that through the Alpha level of mind, I would learn various techniques of problem solving. I liked that and stayed. This course teaches you how to control *your own mind*, using more than the usual 10% of it. It gives techniques to increase memory retention, overcome insomnia, control pain and create healing in the body. At the end of the intensive two weekends, each of us were given a "case study" that presented us with the name and state of a person we had never seen before. We "went to level" and gave all information that came to us about the person. The results were amazing. One man slept through the entire course. Yet, when it came to the case study, he did remarkably well.

This course changed my life. I give it credit for the development of my own intuitive abilities. I was not able to control my mind like I can now. I knew nothing of the Alpha level until I took that class 25 years ago. I even wanted to be a teacher of the Silva method, but they had so many restrictions on the way it could be presented, I gave up the idea. I understand their viewpoint of keeping the teaching more scientific rather than metaphysical so that it could help people of all religious beliefs. But I wanted people to know they were not just a mind and body, but spirit as well. I wanted people to know about their guardian angel. I decided to develop my own method that would combine the scientific *with* the spiritual.

The angels always have an agenda for me that I don't know about. I didn't know that my experiences with the Silva method of mind control would lead me to teach these basic ideas of relaxation and visualization. After study of many different religions, I found these techniques have been around for centuries. Step by step, my angels have led me to this moment.

Third: You Are A Physical Body

Most of us take this wonderful mechanism for granted. When you think about it, you have to marvel at the Intelligence of the Universal Mind that set up this physical creation with its trillions of planets and stars waiting for a visit from you or me. Your body is like a universe with its trillions of cells and its 144,000 electrolytes. In fact, one person speculated that perhaps people have misinterpreted the biblical account of only 144,000 who would be "saved." Maybe the real meaning was that in becoming aware of your spiritual body, you lit up the mystical "lytes" and became "perfect, even as your heavenly Father is perfect." Perhaps when we completely eliminate our fears, we light up like a Christmas Tree and are beamed up not by Scotty, but by our guardian angel. Who knows?

But how did you get this particular body? The soul, with the help of its guides and angel, carefully chose your physical body for this lifetime. It decided if it wanted to be male or female, if it would have great intelligence or little, if it would be born into a large family or be an only child, and hundreds of other details.

I like to imagine my soul going to the Star Room in the spirit realm where the angels put all my ideas for a life experience into the Star Computer, (astrology really does work). Then I go to the Viewing Room where there's a giant screen which presents a glimpse of how my life *might be* with potential parents that I can consider. I trust my angels and guides have already programmed into the life's drama some of the attributes and challenges that together we had chosen. After I choose my potential parents, then I go to the "Waiting Room" like a maternity wing of a hospital while the angels prepare the couple for my "birth." They whisper the idea into their minds. . .or maybe they'll trick them into having me. There are "oops babies" as well as "miracle babies," too.

When all the preparations are made and the embryo is growing in my mother's womb, I, as soul, hover around, encouraging my mother and watching the developing fetus. You can imagine the alarm a soul must feel if the mother begins thinking of abortion. The soul will try to talk the mother out of it. It doesn't wish to have all its plans wiped out. But if the mother does abort the child, the soul leaves and goes back home to gather knowledge from even that experience of not being wanted. It studies this for a time but begins the process of searching for a receptive channel into the physical all over again.

I can't help but imagine that my own mother was a reluctant channel for me. Living in poverty with an alcoholic husband, life was not conducive to having children. She already had three sons and probably didn't want another child. Back then, abortion was unthinkable in the Catholic tradition. So she had me on a hot August day at home with a midwife.

I like to play with the idea that my soul had other plans for me, for, (as the story goes), when I was just a wee girl, barely able to walk, I climbed up on my favorite uncle's lap and whispered in his ear, "Daddy, take me home." And he did. My "visits" grew longer until when I was sixteen my aunt and uncle legally adopted me – against my father's wishes. On my brief visits "home," my father would rant and rave in a drunken stupor about those so-and-so's having stolen his only daughter away from him. Little did he know that my soul had probably planned the whole thing even before I was born! I have often wondered how my four brothers survived it. When I visited, I ached for their poverty and pain. But when people later marveled how they had grown up so well in spite of it all, each one becoming successful and prosperous, I knew their souls also had a plan and they have gained much from their experiences.

Fourth: You Are Emotions/Feelings

The *American Heritage Dictionary* defines "emotion" as: "1. An intense mental state that arises subjectively rather than through conscious effort and is often accompanied by physiological changes; 2. a strong feeling: *the emotions of joy, sorrow, reverence, hate, and love.*"

Let's imagine the soul looking down at Earth from its spiritual home. It sees a ball of swirling energy – mostly water. Knowing that it will enter an exciting adventure into emotions, it holds its nose, yells "Geronimo!" and plunges in. When we, our soul and our personality swim in the clear waters of the emotions of love, peace, harmony and joy, we can feel our angel swimming beside us. But when we venture into the murky waters of anxiety, hatred, prejudice, judgment and fear, our angel seems to disappear. It is still with us. It never leaves. *We lose sight of our angel when we surround ourselves with the darkness of negativity.* To become better acquainted with angels, we have to learn to swim in their territory. Following is a list of common statements reflecting the waters that our mind occupies.

The Ocean of Emotions

Waters of fear	Waters of love
1. I hate it when. . .	I find it uncomfortable when. . .
2. I'm afraid that. . .	I think that. . .
3. I'm dying to. . .	I really desire to. . .
4. That just kills me.	I'm uncomfortable with that.
5. He's a pain in the. . .	He's a real challenge.
6. I'll try. . .	I will (will not). . .
7. I can't see how. . .	Please explain.
8. That burns me up.	I'm not comfortable with that.
9. I'm sick and tired of. . .	I refuse to accept. . .
10. I can't stand to. . .	I prefer to. . .
11. Get off my back!	I'm not comfortable when. . .
12. I'm anxious to. . .	I'm excited about. . .
13. Don't forget to. . .	Remember to. . .
14. I can't afford that.	I choose to spend another way.
15. I'm always a day late and a dollar short.	I'm always at the right place at the right time!

Anger

It is only in this physical world that the soul experiences such a variety of emotions. The soul chooses to come here to create through the challenge of fear. It's like choosing a golf course with the greatest number of challenges. In its home of spirit, it only knows unconditional love. The more practice the soul has in the physical, the easier it is to help the personality remember that it is one with Unconditional Love.

When I speak of "fear" many people, especially men, declare they aren't afraid of anything. We could replace the word "fear" with anxiety, envy, greed, avarice, impatience, intolerance, bigotry or anger.

Anger is probably the most misunderstood of all emotions. Many people use anger to control others so they can fill their own needs *that they fear will not be met.* The bullies of the world are in constant fear that they will not be admired or looked up to. Youth gangs are built around the fear that they will not "fit it," or will not be wanted or loved or "look cool." They use fear to control others, intimidating them and "loving" them at the same time.

Not only is anger based in fear, but people suppress it out of fear of losing control and saying or doing things for which they would regret. Many times when I read a person, I find they have developed some kind of illness because of swallowing their anger. For example, one woman had digestive track disorders because she had pushed her anger down without finding a way to get rid of it. Another person had a chronic cough because she needed to "get things off her chest." One man had heart problems because he knew his wife was cheating on him, but didn't want to confront her out of fear of losing her. His heart was "breaking." In another reading, I saw a back problem in a young father who felt the burden of responsiblity too much. He seemed so surprised that I knew not only that he had a slipped disk, but that he felt anxious and depressed about supporting a growing family.

Hagar and Omar have shown me a different view of anger. They call it the "Action Emotion." It sends signals from the body to the mind that it's not comfortable and needs to be balanced. It's like the robot on "Lost in Space," twirling around with lights blinking, calling, "Warning! Warning!" Yet, either we don't believe it's important enough at the moment to make a fuss about it, or we're afraid we'll be misunderstood, or we're afraid we'll hurt someone's feelings, or many other excuses for ignoring our anger. And so we push it down under our hearts and minds and let it fester. The people who "blow up" are like a smoldering volcano that finally erupts. It's the "straw that broke the camel's back" syndrome. Often, the eruption brings more anger and confusion because it is out of proportion to the "crime."

The angels tell us to listen to our body's signals and bring it into balance when we feel the first signs of anger. If someone says something unkind or sarcastic, respond by saying, "Ouch! That stings!" or "I can see you're impatient with me, but I'm doing the best I can" or "Is there something you'd like to say to me?" This clarifies the real intention behind the words, clearing the air *immediately*. Take a deep breath, see the situation in rainbow lights and choose love. When you seek a win/win outlook, you gain mutual respect and understanding – and it will keep your body healthy.

"But Betty Rae, what if you can't do anything about it? The anger and frustration can't help but build up." You're right. The feeling of helplessness at being unable to change a situation does build up anxiety and can result in smoldering anger, illness, disease and even death. Dr. Carolyn Myss tells of a dentist who developed pancreatic cancer because he felt he couldn't quit his practice even though he hated it. He felt the heavy responsibility of providing for his family. He thought he had no choice, but he did. He chose to stay in dentistry. He died a short time afterward. I find that there are many people who feel chained to their jobs; even though it's destroying their health, they won't quit. *Their fear of financial insecurity drives them to an early grave.*

But there is another way. There are many tricks that will be given thoughout this book on how to avoid anger in the first place. You will learn about going to your "Inner Sanctum" and using your playful imagination to find solutions and peace in any situation. You will learn how to relax and avoid stress. You will learn breathing techniques that can balance you and keep you calm and peaceful. You can begin now by letting go of your expectations of others as the first step in avoiding the discomfort of anger. When you expect others to behave in a certain way and they don't, anger is the result. By accepting people as they are, you're halfway home.

We are all a fragment of God, that incredible Life Force that moves through us, creating us anew each moment. We *are* God expressing beauty and joy in the physical world. We are a co-creator with God in learning how to use Divine Energy to create our personal world.

Five Steps To Your Inner Sanctum
Step One: Lower Brain Waves to Alpha Level
Relaxation

The first step on your journey inward is to relax the mind and body. During these busy days of high stress, people tend to hold a great deal of tension. It causes most of the illnesses you have within the body and almost all of your "headaches." You have to deliberately concentrate on eliminating stress and relaxing your body to heal yourself. Physicians suggest exercise as a way of reducing stress. They are also beginning to suggest meditation. There have been studies that have shown how meditation reduces high blood pressure and prolongs life. I've found that one basic element of relaxation is focusing the mind on each part of the body from the toes to the eyebrows. This keeps the left side of the brain busy – the part of you that wants to analyze everything. By calmly directing the mind's attention to each muscle and gently pulling it back from distraction, the whole body begins to slow down and relax. This is demonstrated on side one of the tapes. As you become accustomed to this exercise, you can relax your mind and body more easily without going through the entire relaxation technique.

Deep Breathing

The second most important element in relaxation is deep breathing. Most people don't know how to breathe. "Of course I know how to breathe. If I didn't, I'd be dead!" you exclaim. I know you think that you already know how to breathe, but my experience as a vocal music teacher says otherwise. When I ask people to take a long deep breath, they suck in their gut, raise their chest and their neck bulges. That tenses rather than relaxes the entire body. A deep breath is neither seen nor heard. You simply open the lungs and sip in breath that reaches down to the diaphragm. This little muscle expands and causes the abdomen to swell. When you exhale, you tighten the stomach muscles to control the flow of air through the vocal cords.

Deep breathing is like food to the body. It sends vital oxygen that energizes and fuels it. The blood carries the oxygen through the walls of the lungs into the red blood cells that carry it throughout the body. When you release the breath, it expels carbon monoxide and water. The process of deep breathing helps to calm you during chaotic moments. Anytime you find yourself in a stressful situation, draw in a deep, calming breath and notice the difference. Deep breathing is essential for relaxation and meditation. These two together open the doors to your Inner Sanctuary.

A simple exercise to build your ability to breathe deeply is to pretend you have a straw in your mouth and you're sipping air. Do this to a count of five, hold the breath to a count of five and then release the air to a count of five. The counting should be similar to the pace of your heartbeat. Practice breathing in for longer counts, holding longer and releasing longer. Remember to relax the body and be sure the neck and shoulders remain down and loose.

There is another way to help you feel what a deep breath is like. Lie on the floor with a sheet of paper on your abdomen. Breathe deeply and watch the paper move. Notice that the shoulders do not move. Feel how this relaxes the body and soothes the mind. You can also do this by standing with your back to a blank wall. Press your shoulders back and then pant like a dog. You'll feel the abdomen move. Then take a deep breath, keeping the shoulders pressed against the wall. You'll begin to feel the right way to breathe.

Practice deep, slow breathing during a confrontation with someone. As you breath out, pretend you are blowing Divine Love toward the person who is upset. See that person surrounded by a cloud of pink energy. Say to them *silently,* "I release you to your greatest good." It doesn't matter that you'd like to strangle him or her. Say again *silently,* "Only good can come to you and only good can be with you." Watch for a small miracle.

Deep breathing brings serenity in the midst of chaos. It can balance the positive and negative energy that surrounds you daily. It can increase your energy when you feel drained. Below are four simple techniques that are given by Joseph J. Weed in his book, *Wisdom of the Mystic Masters*, (Parker Pub. Co., 1968).

The first exercise can reduce stress-related ailments like a simple headache or indigestion. Or if you have been around an emotionally draining individual, this will recharge your batteries.

Breathing Technique #1: Counterbalance a Negative

1. Sit erect, hands loosely on lap, feet separate and planted firmly on the floor.
2. Form a triangle with index, middle finger and thumb by placing them together.
3. Relax deeply, take a deep breath and hold it for 7 counts. Rest.

Repeat seven times.

4. Put the whole thing out of your mind.

5. If you do not find results after two hours, repeat the procedure.

Breathing Technique #2: Counterbalance a Positive

This second breathing technique will counterbalance an overly positive reaction. For example, if you're excited about a long-awaited event that is about to happen, you will not be able to think objectively about it. This exercise will clear your mind.

1. Sit erect, feet touching and firmly planted on floor.

2. Place the fingertips of each hand together and hold them at chest level.

3. Relax deeply, close your eyes and breathe deeply. Exhale for a count of five slowly.

4. Rest for five or six breaths and relax.

5. Repeat #3 and #4 five times.

6. Put the exercise out of your mind.

The nice thing about these first two exercises is that it doesn't matter which you use. If you're not sure, use them both!

The next two techniques are wonderful for a boost of energy. Much better than a chocolate bar – maybe not as yummy, but far less calories!

Breathing Technique #3: Increase Healing Energy

1. Sit erect and relaxed, jaw firmly clenched and hands in a fist.

2. Take a deep breath to a count of five.

3. Relax deeply, take a deep breath and hold it for 7 counts. Rest. Repeat seven times.

4. Imagine each breath bringing a great surge of energy and power which you are storing within you.

Breathing Technique #4: Increase Healing Energy

1. Sit erect and relaxed with feet touching and hands clasped in your lap.

2. Visualize the sun, a great white, flaming orb of prodigious energy, and go there in spirit.

3. Let the sun's tremendous energy flow through your entire be-ing, invigorating and strengthening every particle.

4. After one minute, return to your body, rise and go on with your day.

These simple breathing and visualization exercises balance your energy and create a sense of inner peace. This is the first step in going inward. The more you practice deep breathing, the more natural it becomes. The most important thing to remember is that your breath can be a source of healing to yourself and others. Think of calm, deep breathing as the act of drawing the God Source into your being and exhaling Its healing balm to the world. Use the imagination to create love and peace for Earth.

Relaxation is the most important step toward your Inner Sanctum. You use those newly-learned deep breaths to carry you into deep relaxation of both mind and body. You have a very active mind that never seems to shut up. That was one of the hurdles I had to overcome in order to meditate. No matter how hard I tried to make my mind blank, something would creep in to tease me. I remember picturing a blank movie screen. I tried to hold on to that thought, but soon I saw a fly crossing the screen and had to burst out laughing. But I was ahead of myself. First I had to relax my mind and my body while taking deep breaths.

Step Two: Use the Imagination
Right- or Left-Brain Dominance

The angels speak to you through images, ideas and feelings. These come to you from the right lobe of the brain. It's where you see pictures and visions. Most people are left-brain dominant, which means that they are logical, factual and verbal. One who is right-brain dominant is visually-oriented, artistic, intuitive and impulsive. There is a simple test I use with people to determine which brain dominates. It's not 100% accurate, but fairly close. Follow these simple steps to test yourself:

1. With a pencil, punch a hole in the center of a paper plate.
2. Hold the plate with both hands an arm's length away.
3. With both eyes focus on an object across the room.
4. Close the right eye. If the object disappears, you are left brain dominant because you focused with the right eye. If the object remained, you focused with the left eye and you are right-brain dominant. Whichever eye you focus with, it is the opposite lobe of the

brain that is dominant.

Right-Brain Activities: Personality receives messages from Soul as thoughts, ideas, pictures and feelings. It accepts messages from all the senses without judgment or emotion.

Left-Brain Activities: Personality takes messages from Soul and processes it either from a State of Love, creating comfort in the body or from a State of Fear, creating discomfort in the body. Left Brain sorts, labels, judges and evaluates all messages received from the five senses.

An example explaining brain dominance would be in taking directions. One who is left-brain dominant takes verbal directions and is able to find the place. One who is right-brain dominant would probably have you draw a map, and then would turn it upside down if going south to know whether to turn right or left.

If you are very left-brain dominant, you will have more trouble with visualization. You expect to "see" something behind the eyelids when you close your eyes. Remember, it is the imagination that creates images within the mind's eye. It is not a mirage or a solid substance, but a picture in the mind. When you let go of analyzing everything with words and simply attempt this, you will succeed. Left-brain people are very verbal. They always have words to describe everything. Many people are both left- and right-brain oriented. They can use both sides as needed. Consequently, they can be both creative, innovative and practical. They make great inventors and creative problem-solvers.

Most people believe they can't visualize. A woman came to me for a reading and complained that she had even taken a course in visualization and "didn't learn a thing!" I asked Martha to think of a tree. I waited a moment and asked, "What kind of a tree is it?"

She responded with a shrug, then blurted, "A pine tree."

"Does it have long or short needles?" I probed.

"Long needles," Martha decided.

"Pretend you have a video camera on your tree and as you back away from that close-up of the needles, you can observe where that tree is. Describe what surrounds it.

"It's in my backyard!" she quickly responded with surprise.

None of you have shut your eyes, but each of you has seen that tree. The act of visualizing is simply to bring to mind an object and observe it. This is how you solve problems. You imagine or picture different solutions and "see" how they might turn out. Then you choose the one that seems to work best. The better you are at visualization, the more successful you are at problem-solving.

You have a great library of pictures that your mind recognizes. Words or language trigger those pictures in your mind and instantly release them. This is why you use adjectives to increase the details of a picture. For example, Martha saw a tree. With questioning, the picture evolved from "tree" to a "long-needled pine in her backyard." The more descriptive words you can attach to the picture, the clearer the picture becomes. If you look through a microscopic lens on close-up, you won't know what you're looking at. By taking in details around an object, it comes into focus better. The purpose of this detail in your journal writing is so a long time from now, when you reread it, you will remember and understand. It is very discouraging to go back and get a glimpse of something that doesn't make sense anymore. You defeat the purpose of journal writing, which is to record glimpses of your soul to gain a better understanding of who you really are.

Another important ingredient in visualization is playful imagination. It is an ability to search for alternatives. Most people limit their choices between two things. In their anxiety to find a solution, they tense up and close off their angel's ability to help them. A relaxed body and a playful imagination open up a third solution that you hadn't thought of before. Imagination gives you permission to conjure up silly pictures that lighten up a serious concern and enable you to see from a different viewpoint.

For example, a young client named Steve came to me for a reading to ask how to solve his financial difficulties. He was in his early twenties and didn't even own a car. He had to have a friend bring him. He was considering bankruptcy. Steve was confused about the use of visualization. He explained how he had been visualizing a new red Fiero with special hub caps, power steering, sunroof – the works. He said he even had a picture of it posted on the refrigerator. He'd been working on this for weeks and nothing happened.

I apologized for laughing, but explained to him that he had this thing about visualization all wrong. You don't *tell God and your angels* what you want, you *ask* humbly and politely. Yes, you create your own world, but you have to look for the contradictions in your thinking that keep you from your goals. As I began the reading, I asked his angels for wisdom regarding his financial circumstances. I was shown that his credit cards were at maximum, that he had borrowed from all his friends, including the one who brought him. He seemed to be living two lives – one of great abundance and one of great poverty. Then the angels revealed that he was having "bleed through" from a previous life when he had been very rich. He hadn't accepted the reality of his new circumstances and continued to live beyond his means of income. Once this was revealed to him, he was able to conceive of a new plan of economic responsibility.

First, his angels suggested bankruptcy was not the best way out of his problems. If he was to grow spiritually from his experience, he would have to accept responsibility for his actions. Besides, I explained, "What goes around, comes around." Did he really want to go through all this again in another lifetime? He decided he did not. But he hadn't the foggiest notion how he would get out of his mess. . .especially with the power of visualization.

Simply picturing the vivid details of your desires does not create them. Rather you are to focus on *the end results.* I know most people have been taught to be specific in their goals, but they're misguided. It doesn't work that way. When you try to fill in all the details, you *limit those powerful angelic beings and tie their hands.* Rather, you can write down the *outcome* of what you desire, spoken in spiritual ideas rather than specifics. For example, Steve was to hold in his mind a visualization of himself in a job he enjoyed, easily paying his bills with enough left over for some of the pleasures in life. When he did this, I instructed him not to see himself as rich or winning the lottery, but happy and financially independent.

He also had to conjure up the joyful *feeling* that comes from accomplishing his goals. He could not allow doubt or fear to enter the picture. He could not continue to hold in his mind the negative circumstances that surrounded him now. He was to *bless and thank* God and his angel for presenting him with this challenge and *listen for new ideas* that would change his circumstances.

Next, I suggested he was to take action as he listened to the suggestions that were given from within – or from others, and follow up on them, even if they didn't seem to go anywhere. He had to trust that each step took him to the next step. He had to have trust in his angel. Maybe one interview that didn't pan out was a spiritual exercise to help him overcome his fear of interviews. Once he accepted the challenge and overcame it, he would have accomplished one part of the whole picture that was beyond his understanding, but not for his angel or his soul.

Steve began with some practical steps to lift himself out of his financial bind. First, he cut up his credit cards. Next, he went to each of his creditors and explained his situation, saying he would give a minimum amount to show his good faith until he could obtain a better-paying job. They all agreed.

When Steve reported back to me many weeks later, he revealed a piece of the puzzle that really gave me thrills. He explained that his next door neighbor, an elderly widow, had asked for his help with repairs around her home. He agreed and when she tried to pay him, he refused. He believed he shouldn't take money to help a friend and told her so. His friend then suggested that Steve use her two-year-old Buick that had been sitting in her garage for over a year since she had had a stroke. She suggested that if he would take her to the doctor and shopping once a week, he could use it whenever he wished. Here was the transportation he had asked for – certainly not what he had expected, but a very good substitute. It enabled him to find a better-paying job. He now worked two jobs as well as earning more money being a "handyman" for people his neighbor sent to him. It seemed his whole life began to turn around. Three years later, Steve called to let me know he had his new car – a bright red Fiero – and it was paid for! He thanked me for encouraging him to listen to his angel. I suspected

Steve had begun the change when he turned away from his own troubles to help his neighbor without thought of return. "One good turn deserves another" tells a whole story in itself.

There are four important ingredients in this story. It took Steve's concentrated effort to unite all four aspects of himself to accomplish his goals. Visualization is only one part of the whole. It took his soul's cooperation and that meant no easy-way-out. It took his mind to visualize and focus on his *end results*. It took his emotions to focus on a joyful outcome and not allow fear and doubt to enter his being. And it took action from his physical body to do the things his mind and soul suggested.

Exercises in Visualization

To practice using the right side of your brain, close your eyes, relax and get comfortable. Go through the relaxation tape if you need to. Then try at least one of the following exercises daily.

1. Picture a wall in your living room, preferably one without windows. In your mind, take any pictures off the wall and move the furniture away. In your hand is a paint roller filled with bright red paint. Cover the wall with this paint. Step back and see your furniture next to it. Does it look good? No? Well, change it to bright purple. "Uck!" You say? Okay, change it to deep mauve. How does that look? Keep changing colors until you can visualize any color easily and clearly. Use a color wheel if you need to.

2. Visualize an orange. Cut it in half and watch the juice run. Taste it. Do this with a lemon. Feel your mouth pucker as you taste it.

3. When you enter a room for the first time, observe it carefully. Then test yourself by closing your eyes and trying to picture the room as clearly as you can. The more you do this, the better you will become.

4. When you see a movie, discuss it with someone, recalling a scene as clearly as you can remember. Do this with commercials on tv. Check yourself when they come around again.

Step Three: Prayer

It has been said that prayer is talking to God. Since time began, people have been talking to an unknown deity that draws their minds and souls. None of us really know who or what God is. He/She/It is addressed by numerous names. Some people, whose prayers of petition are ignored, decide that there is no God. Their anger at what happens in their lives is directed at a supreme being "somewhere up there" who is supposedly responsible for all their bad luck. Indeed, through the centuries, most superstition has arisen because of the feeling of helplessness before "the powers that be."

The concept of prayer varies with each individual. It can become rather confusing when you consider how many different religions there are in the world. Each will tell you that its formula for prayer is correct and "the only way." Many people have prayers that are a form of repetitious chant where the sound of the words are more important than their meaning. For example, many eastern religions chant words like "Om" for the resonance of energy that it brings. The Catholic religion honors the mother of Jesus by saying the rosary, using beads to form prayers in groups of ten while meditating on the life of Christ. The hymns sung in churches are said to be prayers said twice because of the power of music added to words. This probably goes back to the ancient belief in chanting like the monks of old. The Benedictine Monks of Santo Domingo de Silos have revived the ancient Gregorian chants in their bestselling recording, *Chant*. The soothing rise and fall of the Latin chant has calmed many in this hectic world.

Many times I have recited the Serenity Prayer to calm me and help me accept the unexpected:

Lord, Grant me the serenity
to accept the things I cannot change,
The courage to change the things I can,
And the wisdom to know the difference.

The most well-known prayer in our western world is "The Lord's Prayer":

Our Father, Who art in Heaven
Hallowed be Thy Name,

Thy Kingdom come, Thy will be done
On Earth as it is in Heaven.
Give us this day our daily bread
And forgive us our trespasses
As we forgive those who trespass against us
And lead us not into temptation
For Thine is the Kingdom, the Power and the Glory
Forever and ever. Amen.

It is believed to be a prayer taught by Jesus. Many have written books about their interpretation of it. I humbly offer my own:

Dear God, who dwells mysteriously within my Soul,
I honor Your Presence.
Make me aware of Your Goodness,
    so that I may hear my Soul's purpose.
Unite within me my physical world
    with Your world of Spirit.
Help me this moment to become aware
    of Your Unconditional Love
So that I may accept myself and others
    as a perfect reflection of your Non-Judgment.
And lead me ever inward toward You and my Soul.
For Your Presence is the Kingdom within,
    reflecting Your Power and Glory forever and ever. Amen.

Probably the most concept-changing prayer for me was one inspired by a NASA scientist who had studied all of the world's religions and saw how similar they were in many ways. He formulated "The Effective Prayer" as a means of focusing his attention on reclaiming his soul from the hectic life that surrounded him. It enabled him to release his prestigious job and retire to the country with his family. He opened a "Light Center" in North Carolina where people came from around the world to pray with him for world peace. He developed his own psychic abilities and was a tremendous help to me during a crisis in my marriage. His work on Earth was completed several years back, but his Center remains. This prayer also helped me release many fears that had been hidden within my heart. Jim concluded that we are all made of God's

"Light." He calls the solar plexus the "Light Center" from which we radiate God to everyone and everything.

The Effective Prayer

by Jim Goure, Black Mountain, North Carolina

I release all of my past, negatives, fears, human relationships, self-image, future, human desires, sex, money, judgment and communication to the Light. I am a Light Being.

I radiate the Light from my Light Center throughout my being.

I radiate the Light from my Light Center to everyone.

I radiate the Light from my Light Center to everything.

I am in a bubble of Light and only Light can come to me and only Light can be here.

Thank You, God, for everything, for everyone and for me.

Step Four: Meditation

Meditation is an area of great confusion. While some people actually fear meditation as a source of evil, most believe that while prayer is *talking to God,* meditation is *listening to God.* And listening, to a lot of people, means shutting off the mind, making it "blank." For me, that's impossible. The mind is a receiver of all kinds of messages from the subconscious feedback of the body, to the super-conscious suggestions from your soul and angel. Add to that the constant flow of energy waves that bombard the conscious mind from the five senses. And you also have to remember that you can pick up thoughts of others without even knowing it. So just what is meditation?

Meditation is an act of focusing attention inward. Meditation is a means of communicating with the Source, God, *through your angel and soul.* Some people expect to hear His voice in deep booming words somewhere outside of themselves. He/She/It rarely, (if ever), speaks directly with you. Instead, your angel and your essence or soul attempt to transmit communication from the Source.

By allowing your playful imagination to take over, you can then flow with what comes. You first have to calm the babble of your mind and release the anxieties of the day in order to be open enough to listen. Through the process of relaxation and concentrated focus of attention, you can receive guidance and knowledge that you didn't have before. You can become all that you can imagine and more.

I have a tendency to oversimplify. Having taught music and English for over thirty years, you do that. Yet, I am always a student as well. In my thirst for mystical knowledge, I've learned that truth isn't complicated. It is simple. We as humans tend to make life very complicated. We want to analyze, scrutinize, categorize, and label every thought, word and deed. We have so many words that mean the same thing, while others can sound the same but have an entirely different meaning. It would be easy to drown in words and ideas. My angels encourage me to keep it simple.

Step Five: Creating an "Inner Sanctum"

At the end of Chapter One, you listened to the tape that led you into your Inner Sanctum. This is the tabernacle of God within you where your spirit and angel dwell. "Sanctum" is a Latin word meaning "holy place." It is a private visual within the mind where one is free of intrusion. It is here that you can find real comfort, unconditional love and complete harmony. Yes, and it is right *within you*. You learn that you don't need to search for a "soul mate" to become "complete." You're already complete because you're one with your soul, your angel and God. It is your conscious mind in a physical body that sees only a fraction of truth and is capable of understanding only a fraction of the whole.

Negative thoughts and feelings often block you from entering your Inner Sanctum. As you begin to really listen to yourself, you pick up the negative programming that has gotten you stuck in certain habits of behavior. For example, if you had parents who were overly critical and judgmental, you may tend to be that way also. Yet, you may resent anyone who criticizes or judges you.

Summary

You may say, "But I am what I am," or "How do you expect me to change at my age?" First of all, I impose no expectations upon you for I've come to learn that you are perfect just the way you are at this moment in time. Each of you do the best you can with what you know. But your soul, or spirit-self, is *always striving to grow through new experiences and new knowledge*. It is always encouraging you to become all that you can be. Until you respond to this urging, you cannot begin to know the wonderful things you can accomplish. Until you open your mind and heart to new ideas, you cannot respond at all.

Most people are usually so busy with everyday concerns that they aren't even aware of who they are or where they are going let alone recognize their souls or especially their angels. It's like they're sailing their boat without any compass or rudder. Then one day they wake up and ask, "What is life all about? Why am I here? What's the purpose of it all? There's got to be more to life than this!"

It is then that you begin searching. You search here and there and can't seem to find God anywhere. You cry out to Him and feel ignored. Then one day, you grow very quiet and from deep within you hear, "Beloved, I am here," and you feel a wash of wondrous love flow over and through your person. You take a deep breath and joy fills every cell. And you *know*.

But, too quickly, you forget that euphoric moment and find yourself back in your daily routine, feeling frustrated and lost all over again. Your soul has agreed to create a veil of amnesia as to who you really are as part of your experience in the physical. You, the *personality,* spend your lifetime discovering *who you are!* You don't remember past lives because they'd scare you too much. You don't remember your soul, because you can't see it. You don't even remember God until your angels wake you. Then you have this restlessness to discover who you are, where you're going and where you came from. For those of you reading this book, you have searched long and wide before now and you're still questioning. Sometimes you think you've found the answer, but, *poof*, it vanishes like a wisp of smoke. Your angels whisper the answer and you grasp it hungrily, but time passes and you've lost it once more.

The Real You

*A Personality with a Physical Body
with Emotions and Feelings,
Mind and Intelligence
That is within a Soul
That is a Divine Spirit
within All That Is – God.*

Your journal will help you unravel these revelations and tie them down long enough for you to hold on to them to study and make them your own. Without a recording of these thoughts and impressions, you simply forget.

The angels and I will guide you through a second visualization where you will meet your guardian angel once again. Remember that you are seeing with your playful imagination. You will not "see" it in vivid Technicolor detail – at first. Maybe you won't actually "see" anything, but you may sense something or you may *imagine* what it looks like. Let your mind create the scene without judging or analyzing. Let it flow and enjoy it. It will take you step-by-step toward your Inner Sanctum.

Journal Entries for Week Two

Directions: Throughout the week, listen to side two of the tapes that accompany this book. It will take you through a relaxation and visualization. Let your playful imagination lead you where it will. Trust that your angel will guide you perfectly. When you have finished, record what you saw and felt.

1. Use "The Effective Prayer" on page 42 to help you remember the visualization with your guardian angel. Write all your impressions immediately after listening to the tape.

2. Practice "Breathing Technique #1: Counterbalance a Negative" on page 33 whenever you feel the need.

3. When feeling rushed and harried, pause, take a deep breath and enter your Inner Sanctum. Picture your guardian angel and feel love and peace surrounding you. Do this at least once a day. Record impressions and results in your journal.

4. Begin recording your opinions and beliefs in your journal. Observe the times your opinions caused you to act or react in a certain way. If you are not comfortable with your reaction, take it to your angel in your Inner Sanctum and ask for help.

5. Get in the habit of counting backwards to program your body to relax until you can count backwards from 3 to 1 and immediately be in your Inner Sanctum.

6. Practice deep breathing during times of stress. Memorize the breathing techniques so you can try them during the day. Pay close attention and record the results.

7. Write a description of the four parts of who you are: Soul/Spirit; Mind/Intelligence; Emotions/Feelings; Body/Action. Pay close attention this week so you can record your thoughts and emotions. Refer to this chapter for ideas.

8. Begin to notice which of the four parts of you respond first to a situation. Do you mull it over and over (mind)? Do you feel it in your gut first (emotions)? Do you act first and then think about it later (body/action)? Or do you pray about it first before you act (spirit)?

9. After you have written in your journal for a few days, reread it and look for insights into your soul's purpose for your life. Observe your anxieties and complaints. How can you change them for good? How do they express your inner desires?

10. Pay close attention to each activity one day. Focus all of your attention on the moment, being determined to see the good in it – from an angel's perspective. Observe how this makes the day flow.

Chapter 3
Why Am I Here?

Dear Guardian Angel, hear my call.
What is the purpose of it all?
Why am I in this world of woe?
What did I do to make it so?

"Beloved Child, Be still and hear:
You are greatly loved. I am always near.
Your Purpose is to love all that you think and do.
It will bring peace and joy to you."

This past week, you practiced going within through relaxation and visualization. You gave yourself time to get acquainted with this technique of meditating so that it is becoming easier for you to go within. This week builds upon the last and opens your mind to your purpose for being here.

To even begin to understand your purpose in life, it is important you realize that you are a multidimensional being; you live simultaneously in the physical world as well as in the astral and higher realm of soul. All have an effect on you. The more you become aware of all the nuances of energy that confront you, the more you will be able to control your own life and realize your purpose for being here. Each dimension has its own purpose for what happens in your life.

For example, you meet someone to whom you are instantly attracted. On a soul level, you respond to the awareness of another soul with whom you've had previous happy encounters. Your souls were probably setting up this encounter before your lives even began. Sometimes this "chance meeting" seems to be an amazing set of coincidences. You "just happen" to know a person who "just happens" to know someone. They set you up. It clicks. This soul-level recognition draws you together. In the beginning, you seem to have so much in common. Perhaps you marry. Little by little, you become disillusioned. You have expectations of your partner that are not filled. You realize that your partner is also disenchanted. On and on the tale is told on every soap opera ever created.

In one reading, I discovered that the reason a woman's marriage had grown dull was that she and her husband had been comrades in arms, playing the "Three Musketeers" in another lifetime. They had had so much fun together being the macho Prince Vallients, running around the countryside on their brave stallions, saving every damsel in distress, that they really wanted to return to the "good old days." But their angels and souls played a trick on them. It made them male and female and drew them into marriage. They tried the party circuit, going to bars together and entertaining in their home. But they became bored with each other and before long, were having affairs with others. Each suspected it, but it didn't seem to bother them. "That's life!" they believed.

When the woman asked me what she should do, I shook my head because I couldn't answer. When I asked her angel, there was silence. Nothing more was given. It had shown her situation quite clearly; now it was up to her to decide what to do with it.

It was about three months later when the woman made another appointment. She had done some "soul searching" and after discussing the reading with her husband, they had decided to make the best of it. They agreed that they were best friends and enjoyed each other's company. They figured it was time they grew up and quit playing. They decided to have a family.

The Pendulum of Opposites

To understand your many purposes in life, we'll begin with the physical world and its confusing opposites. For example, just when you get used to summer, if you live in a climate-changing world, it goes away and plunges you into the snowy cold of winter. For those who have migrated to warmer climates, you have traded tornadoes for hurricanes and snow for rain and floods. Mother nature seems to be a study of opposites.

And people can be confusing as well. Just when you think

you know someone, *bam!* They change. Probably people are the most confusing basket of opposites you will ever encounter. And because people are one of the main reasons why you're here, we'll take some time to figure them out.

In the previous chapter, we spoke of "The Ocean of Emotions" in which you can find yourself close to drowning now and then. People will ask, "Why am I having so much trouble? What am I doing wrong?" They assume that if they could only learn the reason behind their difficulty, they could have a life free of emotional pain. That just isn't part of physical reality. While in this dimension, you're going to experience the whole gambit as the pendulum swings first to the right and then to the left.

Create a playful picture of yourself joyously swimming in that Ocean of Emotions. See the water clear and glistening like diamonds. Then you can become aware of the purpose behind each experience. But when you dwell in anxiety, those waters become cloudy. Throughout life, while spirit wears a physical body, it cannot escape swimming in those murky waters of fear. This is part of the challenge your soul takes on with that body. You live on a planet that has positive and negative polarities. But often in your anxiety to "figure it out," you tend to believe that anything negative is "bad." Some people can go to extremes in this belief and find themselves trapped in those dark waters simply because they're too afraid to move into the light.

In fact, a few people are too scared to move at all! Depression is becoming a chronic disease as people sink deeper and deeper into their negative thoughts and feelings of helplessness. You may hear someone say, "Oh, what's the difference?" as they give up their hopes and dreams, which may have been their soul's vision or purpose for their life. Or they may say, "Why try? You'll only be disappointed." Anxiety about failure, of being hurt physically or emotionally, of losing a loved one, or missing an opportunity, and a dozen different things can keep you locked up in the status quo. Many never break out of their self-confined cells of fear. It can feel like swimming in circles in heavy, dark waters.

I remember feeling helpless about my relationship with Todd.

We had both tried to understand the other, but were too often disappointed in unfulfilled expectations. One time after a lengthy argument, I felt so depressed that I began to weep and couldn't stop. I remember curling up in a fetus position on the bathroom floor next to the tub. The tears flowed nonstop. Todd became anxious and then angry with his frustration with me. He didn't know what to do. He even tried slapping me across the face to snap me out of it. But that only made me withdraw and cry even more. It was finally exhaustion that gave me relief. I fell asleep.

Sleep has always been a means of healing for me. I am convinced that my angels lift me up and nurse and heal my soul. They gently set me back on Earth the next morning with a feeling of wondrous love and joy. . .until I remember. Then my mind goes into overdrive, trying to figure out, "What to do? What to do?"

Imagine life as your soul gathering experiences in the physical dimension. It is like an artist who creates a portfolio of paintings that express his unique abilities, talents and creativity. Your reactions to life are your own unique portfolio – the sum total of all that you are, including your past life experiences. These reactions include every feeling, thought, belief, action and reaction to life. If you become too steeped in the negative pull of the planet and get stuck in the waters of fear, you won't venture out to try new ideas. Your soul becomes disappointed, creating a restlessness within you that won't go away.

Balance

The key is **to balance the positive with the negative by being neutral or detached**. This doesn't mean being lethargic, uncaring or indifferent. It means a willingness to let go of your way of viewing a situation and let your angel show you another.

Dr. Carlos Warter writes of this balance in his book *Recovery of the Sacred: Lessons in Soul Awareness*, (Health Communications, 1994). In it he says, "I found my meditations often gravitated toward this process of reconciling opposites. As I entered soul awareness, ideas that seemed at odds with each other – love and hate, change and satisfaction, giving and receiving – would blend into a feeling that these two were really expressions of the same principle. I came to realize that there were no polarities possible in the realm of spirit. When opposites become harmonious paradoxes, it was another sign that I had connected with my soul. In addition to a sense of timelessness and universal love, I knew I was in a state of soul awareness when I felt comfortable with paradoxes."

Many people believe they have to overcome all their negative tendencies and become positive. Some even believe the flesh is evil and the cause of our downfall. But let's not throw out negative energy entirely. We need both positive and negative energy to survive, to recreate the energy from which we draw life. Just as a battery has both positive and negative poles, so do we. As an analogy, we could use the idea of electricity with the need for "neutral grounding" to keep our light burning. It is only sensible to look at the pros and cons of any situation. For example, it is unethical of news reporters to slant a story with their own opinions and feelings. Yet, this is happening all the time. Our television news broadcasting is slanted toward the negative side of life, showing us everything from murder and rape to natural disasters. We need to become aware of that imbalance and not allow it to create an imbalance within ourselves through lethargy and depression.

The way most people create imbalance in their lives is through beliefs and opinions. They tend to seek out experiences that will support their opinions and ignore any that contradict it. We want to believe something in print when it shows a "fact" to prove our point. No so. That article may just be another person's opinion.

Teaching my Language Arts students the difference between fact and opinion was one of my most difficult tasks. Kids would say, "I hate school and that's a fact!" We hunted through magazine advertisements for real facts and found mostly opinions. Only Quaker Oatmeal gave a few facts about the advantages of fiber content. The rest told you how beautiful or sexy or relieved you would be by using their product. Ads claim they are "80% better than (another product)." What fact is that? They say "doctors recommend" their product. So a doctor likes it; what fact is that? Now that edible products are required to be labeled, we have more facts about food, but even with that, you have to watch out. Whenever they talk about percentages, they can fudge the facts. Percentage of what? "Total daily requirements?" What requirements? Who says so?

And the scientific community claims research says this and research says that. We're all growing a little weary of the contradictions research comes up with. First, butter is bad for us and then it's not. Next, eggs are bad for us and then they're not. When we talk about research, we have to ask, "Who's doing the research?" "Who stands to gain?" I know it sounds cynical, but with the world mad for the "bottom line" of profit, there is just too much slanted reporting even in the so-called scientific community. My son, Josh, might have a problem with this, but even he tells of his colleagues who try to quote "facts" when he knows of research that contradicts it, or he can prove that they have misquoted their source.

So what does it all mean? It means that *neutral grounding enables us to view both the positive and negative poles without getting caught up in fear. . .of being deceived. . .of being "ripped off". . .of not having all the facts.* **And that neutral position comes from our angels.** They help us view what we see and read with a better handle on the difference between fact and opinion. They help us evaluate commercials from that neutral position that doesn't have an opinion looking for verification. They also help us to trust that inner knowledge we receive. Once we let go of trying to prove something, we can trust our angels who have all the facts.

Negative experiences are part of life. No one sails through life without something "bad" happening, without some disappointment, failure and upset. Imagine how boring our life would be if there were no challenges and adventures. When we look for the good in all things, these so-called "negative experiences" become neutral and even positive. The following is a practical example from my own life.

In my first marriage, I had always been pulling in the positive side of life while Todd was pulling in the negative. In trying to balance one another, we were both out of balance. Todd saw me as naive and unrealistic, always looking for the "good" in everyone and everything. He believed it was better to see life as it really was and to quit fooling myself. Our imbalance made it impossible to communicate.

The process of divorce is an emotional rollercoaster ride. When it ended, I was determined to remain single for the rest of my life. I was joyful and content. I no longer had to go home to arguments, criticism and ridicule. But my soul and angels were scheming behind my back. They had other plans. Two years after, they inspired Fran, a student of mine in 1956, to give Joe my picture.

It took Joe Calleja two months to work up enough nerve to call me. He had been widowed for eight years and many women had tried to latch onto this gentle man. He was fed up with being manipulated and simply wanted someone to accompany him to the theater. He loves opera. He didn't know I was a music teacher.

When I first met Joe, my reaction was, "My God, he's short!" I'm five-foot-three and we met nose to nose. Although I felt drawn to this man, I didn't want to get serious. I didn't want to become involved. I refused to ever let any man rule my life again! But, on the other hand, we did have fun together. He seemed more of a 'man' than any I'd ever met. He didn't have to be macho or try to manipulate. He knew his own mind, yet was able to listen and appreciate my thoughts and opinions. I enjoyed our intellectual banter. I loved his light-hearted sense of humor. (The angels were reeling us in!)

We both tried to size up one another from a neutral position, putting the plus and minus attributes on a list in our minds. When the pros began to outweigh the cons, and we realized that we each had found a gem, we slid off that neutral position into fear, like sliding down a hill into a puddle of muck. The fear of losing control of the situation was paramount.

Meanwhile, Joe wasn't interested in getting serious either. But soon his scales began to slide more toward the positive. He reasoned, "I'm really beginning to like her, but she's still dating someone else. What if we become involved and her ex-husband comes back? Maybe I should get out of this before I'm in too deep."

The pendulum was swinging from positive to negative until our angels stepped in and "grounded" us. They began opening our thoughts to one another, increasing our ESP at an amazing rate. They kept us in neutral while we observed one another. They encouraged us to let go of the fear that could have gotten us stuck in the negative and clouded our thinking. They continued to whisper to us the other's thoughts and set us to wondering just what was going on.

It only took us six months to decide to be married. After seven years, we're still able to stay neutral in expressing our needs and desires while our love and respect for one another grow stronger. Joe comments how much he loves the freedom this gives. He says he can reveal his innermost thoughts without fear, and it's wonderful. It's just letting the other person "be." I agree.

After sharing my thoughts about this book, Joe gave another example of staying neutral through the concept of magnetism. We know that our bodies are made up of an electromagnetic field of positive and negative energy. He said we are like a light bulb in the middle of that field. When we balance that plus/minus energy, we turn on our light. And *if we pull in too much negative energy, the bulb dims. And if we pull in too much positive energy, the bulb also dims.* We need "grounding" or balance. And to obtain that, we learn to look at the negative things of life from a neutral viewpoint.

We often create imbalance from reliving past experiences. When you pull in a painful memory, your mind creates the pain of it all over again. But if you review the experience from a neutral, detached position, you can see the good that has come from it. You can turn a negative experience into knowledge and wisdom. It then becomes an asset in your life. And as with all energy, positive, negative or neutral, it is never wasted.

When we can use negative energy in a neutral way, balancing it with the positive, we can become better decision makers and have more control over our lives. In working out an intricate problem like building a house, one has to look for the negative consequences of any positive action. For example, if you decide to move a wall, you have to figure where your support beams are, and if they need that wall to keep the roof from falling. When you weigh the positive and negative reactions of someone with whom you must negotiate, you are looking ahead at possibilities and probabilities. You look at the pros and cons of a situation from a *nonjudgmental, neutral position*. This is an essential factor in good decision making.

An example of leaning too far into the positive zone could be in deciding upon the purchase of a new home. If you bought one just because it was pretty and didn't bother to check out the structure and foundation, or to see if the roof leaks, or to investigate the best interest rates and payments, you could create a great deal of headaches in the future. You have to check out the negative side of life *from a neutral position* – not one of fear. *It is always a matter of balance.*

The State Of Fear

In Chapter Two, we touched upon the Ocean of Emotions. In this chapter, we will look at fear as a state of being rather than an emotion. *The State of Fear* has many disguises. It's known as anxiety, restlessness, envy, greed, avarice, anger, lack and all the other negative feelings on the Pendulum of Opposites, found on page 69. You may believe you are simply reacting to a person or situation and do not realize how you've plunged yourself into the icy waters of fear. One student, Dana, said she wasn't afraid of anything. Her concept of fear was tied up with it's opposite – bravery.

But we're not talking about being brave here, or of facing issues or people. We're talking about those anxieties and inhibitions that you, most often, aren't even aware of. When this lady related an incident when she "jumped all over her friend's case," she was amazed she had reacted the way she did. Getting beneath the surface, we discovered that Dana had an issue with being understood – with intelligent communication. She often felt impatient with people who didn't know what she was talking about. She felt she needn't explain. "They should know." But they didn't. This new knowledge opened her mind to many other possibilities where fear could sneak up on her.

Which state of being you choose begins with your *reaction* to a thought, word or action. For example, you may react with anger to a statement made to you because you believed it was either untrue or unjust. What you were really fearing is that you might be misunderstood or criticized or made to "look bad." When you detach from your need to be loved, praised and appreciated, you will not react with fear. When you look within for that Perfect Love *and find it*, you feel secure and well-loved. That is quite a tall order for most of us, but it begins with simply recognizing which form of fear you are experiencing and then choosing to love instead. Choose to love the person who is criticizing you. You're laughing! I'm laughingly serious. This is what is meant by turning the other cheek. You allow that person to be the best they can be in the present moment. Perhaps that person is acting out of a need to control his own life, believing it is gained through power over others. Perhaps that person needs love and praise and feels threatened by you. Search for the good in a person and find a "perhaps" that may be the exact fit.

Control is a big factor for many people. Because of anxiety about the bad that *might happen,* people may try to manipulate others and events around them. Their belief system is quite rigid and in order to stay in control, they often impose their beliefs on others. Because this never works, these people are often frustrated and angry. They tend to blame everyone and everything – except themselves – for their "failures." They have a great need to "look good" in other people's eyes because they fear they really aren't good enough. Criticism is often their tool of control and the hardest for them to receive. Emotions are close to the surface in people who have a need to control. They often feel unappreciated and react with anger to oversights from others.

Worry is one of the biggest reasons for people to be caught in the emotion of fear. There are "born worriers." They worry about the weather, friends, relatives, wars, etc. They can find a dozen things to worry about all at once. They almost love to worry, seeking out problems in others to worry about when their own life is dull. They even become addicted to soap operas so they can worry about the characters playing in them. Worry becomes such a habit that it seems almost impossible to break. Yet, if they wish to hear their angel and to know inner peace and joy, they will begin to change this debilitating habit.

All the habits you have created began with a need you were trying to fill. It feels like a nagging worry within the gut that seeks an ease to its pain. For example, I remember counseling one older woman who worried she would lose her husband who was not well. She feared being alone, of being unable to take care of herself. She worried about her own health, of becoming so ill that she couldn't take care of him. She worried about the finances of a long illness. Many a night she laid beside her husband who slept peacefully while she worried about him, becoming angry with him for not worrying with her. She felt she was being "practical" in her worrying. And indeed, it is *okay* to be *concerned about* illness and death, but when it became an *obsession* with something that *may never happen,* she was going way beyond simple concern.

Here's where balance comes in. It begins with trust in your angel to take care of those things over which you have no control. Yes, it is practical to have insurance to cover long-term illness. Yes, it is practical to take care of your health on a day-to-day basis. You do what can be done and then leave the rest to God.

It seems to me that worry is a basic lack of trust in God. Perhaps it's almost a fear of God – a belief that you may be punished if you're not "good." Worry is a belief in disaster lurking around the corner, ready to pounce on us at any moment. *The anecdote to worry is trust that good will come from any experience, even a seeming disaster.* Although we are "Light Beings," as humans we can block that light through fear. We cloud it with doubt, worry, anxiety, apprehension, suspicion, concern and dread. How often we say, "I'm afraid that. . .," "I'm worried about. . .," "What if. . .," "I know I should. . .," "If only he would. . .," or "I dread. . ."

Emmanuel quips, "Ask your higher wisdom if it is not true that without worry you would have arrived exactly where you are now, and more pleasantly. . .Doubt is the rabbit's foot of fear. Worry and fear are not tickets on the express train. They are extra baggage. You were going that way anyway." (Bantam Books)

How often we dwell on the same mistake or hurt that freezes us in that past moment of time, continuing the same hurt over and over. How often we fear some loss or future calamity that steals away the joy of the present. How often we take for granted those we love, berating them for inconsequential things, putting expectations on them that make them feel guilty or uncomfortable. How often we judge others, deciding what is "best" for them, what they "should" and "should not" do, or be, or feel, or think. And we do it all in the name of 'love.'

Emmanuel speaks playfully about love versus fear, showing the negative pole as a playful imp that loves to scare us. He says, "What does the voice of fear whisper to you? Fear speaks to you in logic and reason. It assumes the language of love itself. Fear tells you, 'I want to make you safe.' Love says, 'You **are** safe.'"

Early Programming

With each experience, you draw conclusions that form your beliefs about life. For example, if you have had a dysfunctional home life, you could come away with many illusions about love. If you were taught that being good brought love and being bad withheld love, you may try to please those from whom you desire love. It gets complicated. But when you realize that love really is the bottom line, you become aware of the patterns you have created.

Everyone has basic needs: nourishment for the body through food, shelter and clothing; knowledge to nourish the mind; the expression of beauty and joy to nourish the emotions; and an awareness of God's Unconditional Love to nourish the soul. Threaten to lose any of these and your body, mind, emotions and soul push the panic button. Consequently, your entire lifetime is spent in fulfilling these basic needs in one way or another. And it is only natural to look to others for those needs. You were trained well in this dependency by being born a helpless infant. You learned daily what you had to do to receive the love, attention, praise and nourishment that you craved. As an infant, you cried when you were hungry or wet. As a child, maybe you whined to get your way; as a teenager, you might have had rages to frighten your parents into giving you your way; as an adult, you may have learned the weapons of praise and criticism, or the giving or withholding of love. Oh, yes, you learned well.

The more I meditated on the "Effective Prayer" (page 42), the more I became aware of all the negative programming I had accumulated over the years. I craved love and attention because I was afraid no one could love me, or that my aunt and uncle may not keep me. I was the "good little girl" and learned quickly to become what others wanted. I soaked up any glimmer of praise and elaborated upon it. If they said I was smart, I studied hard. If they thought I was talented, I practiced long hours. But that left me in fear of failure and more especially in fear of criticism which would mean I wasn't loved. Now I know how futile this belief was, but I didn't as a child.

When I visited my parents and brothers, I tried so hard to please them. My brain scrambled trying to keep up with their bantering and teasing. I learned to play chess because "everyone who's anyone learns to play chess." I never did very well. I felt guilty that I had so many material possessions when they were so poor. I became generous, giving away things just to please and receive their approval and love. My aunt claims that it took me a couple of weeks to become myself again after a visit. I had no idea what she meant then, but I do now.

As a young adult, I still wasn't aware of the negative beliefs that ran my life. I married a man whom I saw as strong and secure. I believed he would take care of me and fill all my needs. He was strong and he did try to fill my needs. But my soul knew I had to eliminate my fears of criticism and my need for praise and approval. Therefore, Todd was the master teacher sent to do the job. He pushed my buttons of fear and stirred up my emotions. He withheld love when he disapproved.

One incident reveals it all. In a happy mood, I threw my arms around Todd and hugged him. He stood with arms at his side, unresponsive. I backed away, hurt and puzzled. I asked, "What's wrong?" He answered as he walked away, "Nothing." I pleaded, "What's *wrong?*" He blurted out some grievance of a task I had either failed to do right or forgotten to do at all. It was said with such anger and condemnation as though I had deliberately done – or not done – this task just to hurt him. I was amazed and felt literally ill. It was like a blow to my midsection. I had to sit down. I didn't understand. I tried to explain. We argued. He found other grievances to throw at me to prove his point. I tried to explain. On and on we went as the push-pull, love-hate game continued.

I'm a slow learner. It took me thirty-two years before I learned from this grand manipulator of emotions. I learned I could not please anyone but myself. I learned I was not responsible for anyone's happiness but my own. I learned I was responsible for each decision I made each moment of my life. I could not blame anyone but myself if my life was not what I desired. When I finally awoke to this wisdom, I ended the marriage. Oh, it wasn't a sudden decision, but rather a slow process of bits and pieces that extended over ten years with marriage counseling and many hours of trying to explain who and what I was. What I didn't know was how well Todd had helped me see myself. I finally figured out how to fill my own basic needs for self-expression and unconditional love.

Mirroring

People are the best way to learn about your soul's purpose in life. You need all kinds who test your patience as they become a mirror to who you really are. In this world of cause and effect, you're constantly reacting to someone. Every person who appears in your life has a gift to give you. It is the gift of yourself. You may choose a partner who may be the direct opposite of who you are. Opposites are a wonderful way to learn your strengths and weaknesses.

Most people believe their purpose is some grand, noble, life-fulfilling work. My son berated me one day saying, "Mom, it's all your fault!" "My fault for what?" I puzzled. "You made me feel I was special and would do something special with my life. But I'm not. . .and I didn't." I smiled and gently replied, "Tony, you are special with your gentle ways and kind heart. You go out of your way to help people and do good for them. You touch many hearts and uplift them with your sincerity and honesty. Life is not lived in the big things you do, but in the little things you say and do each day for one another."

Some people measure their life by their "accomplishments." What is that? Nothing but a reflection of society's materialistic viewpoint of success. If you're not "filthy rich," you're poor. If you're not the corporate president, you've failed. If you're not beautiful/handsome, you're ugly. If you're not witty and smart, you're dull and stupid. How do you measure yourself? What yardstick do you use? Pay close attention to this because it may also reflect your beliefs about your purpose in life. You may have missed the point just as my son did.

How do you define yourself? If you were to answer the statement, "I am. . ." what would you say? Go to your journal and write out as many "I am's" as you can to describe who you are. Be brief. For example, many people identify who they are by their work. You may say, "I'm a factory worker," or "I'm a teacher," or as I've heard some women say, "I'm just a homemaker," as though this most important of jobs were nothing!

Some people identify who they are through a comparison with others. For example, if I were to say, "I'm fairly attractive," I might see myself as "not bad for over 60!" What does that say? It says that I compare myself with other sixty-year-olds, and believe I'm younger looking, well kept, a little overweight, but *"not too bad."* I "see myself" with blond hair that covers gray, makeup to cover wrinkles, stylish clothes that express my personality, etc. I also like long fingernails and *grow them at the beauty parlor!* So – does that make me a fake with dyed hair and artificial nails? If others would judge me so, that's their concern. It certainly isn't mine! I'm doing what pleases me. I radiate joy and happiness. That's what counts.

Do you see how this mirroring reveals to myself who I really am and begins to point out my purpose for being here? I believe my soul selected an "attractive" body type to fulfill its purpose of teaching and public speaking. I wouldn't be much good to my soul if I were so ugly that people would cringe when they looked at me.

I might have a wonderful personality, but as a lecturer, they wouldn't have enough time to get to know me before my appearance had turned them off. Quasi Moto, the Hunchback of Notre Dame, repelled most people – until they got to know him.

The State of Love

How do you play with the angels? Choose love. As I've said before, perhaps I oversimplify. Yet, each day you make the choice between fear or love many times. Every action creates a reaction. You choose how you will perceive that action in the first place. For example, if someone you didn't know called you a name, you probably would disregard it because you wouldn't care what they thought. But if someone you love and admire called you a name, you may believe it and choose to feel hurt, or ashamed, or guilty, or angry. Choose instead to react with love, accepting that the person who said an unkind thing, at best, was trying to help you or really didn't mean it or, at the very least, was rude. You can let go of your fear that they don't admire or love *you*. You can choose to love them just the way they are. You can choose to laugh it off, or you can choose to tell them off. You do have a choice.

The Language of Angels is Spoken
To the Soul through desires, urges and inner drives
to think, speak and act in love;
To the Mind through pictures, words or knowing;
To the Emotions through feelings, intuition and hunches;
To the Body through tingles, butterflies and Joy.

You can get signals from your angel in many different ways: 1) from your soul that sends a silent message to your mind – a desire; an urge; an inner drive to action; 2) from your mind that sends a verbal message through your voice that can amaze you with wit, poetry and wisdom; 3) from your emotions that send warnings of impending danger or excited anticipation; and 4) from your body that sends the signals through butterflies in the stomach, or a headache, or a cold in the head, or many other dis-eases within the body. Often within the body is the last relay of the message that reaches you because you do not listen to the others. Often you have to have a head cold to realize you are stuffing your mind without taking time to sort and store what you are receiving.

A friend had chest congestion for over three weeks. Her doctor said it was allergies, not an infection. I wasn't so sure because she sounded very ill and was coughing chronically. One day, she and her boss had a "knockdown, drag-out fight." "They could hear us three offices away," she laughed. As she was telling me this, I realized how clear she sounded and said, "You really had to get that off your chest, didn't you?" It struck us both with awe as we realized how significant that flippant play on words really was. People do cause most of their own illnesses. Don't misunderstand. Your illnesses are *real* – not psychosomatic. Your body really does run a fever and grow infections. But it does so **for a purpose**. My friend's body tried hard to tell her what her soul had been saying for quite some time: "Stand up for what is right and good for all concerned." That was her soul's purpose in that experience. And it will present many more like it until she figures out what knowledge and wisdom her soul is seeking to gain.

Remember, you are a soul with many *purposes for being here.* . .not just one, but a multitude of purposes with many dimensions of being. To understand the purpose for each encounter, your soul must reach through to your mind, body and emotions to reveal the "why's" behind each experience.

Our Inner Stage

So many times when I'm giving a reading to a chronic worrier, the angels have presented me with a simple technique for eliminating worry. The angels say that worry is like wrapping a loved one in a wet blanket of negativity on a cold day. No one really wants that. Instead, you are to visualize a darkened stage where you are standing on the director's podium with your back to the audience. One by one, picture the people in your life sitting with their instrument that is slightly out of tune with your own personal music. Picture a spotlight of Divine Love flowing over, around and through them. See it like a rainbow of golden champagne bubbles – alive and pulsating like radiant colored lights flowing down, around and through the individual or object of worry. Know that this light is God's Love and say, "I release you to your greatest good. Only good can come to you and only good can be with you." Then also picture the person's guardian angel standing behind him with its wings wrapped around him. Know this loved one is following the Divine Plan for this life perfectly.

Do this one by one for each person who has entered your life story to play on the stage in your drama. After all, you are the conductor, tuning up the instruments (vibrations) of those around you so that your life may be more harmonious. Do this for those you love as well as for those with whom you are having conflict. Worry is a dissonance you do not want. Focus your attention on tuning up the orchestra of your life. When everyone is harmonizing, your own life sings beautifully and serenity surrounds you.

I gave this idea to a man who came for a reading, desperate as to what to do about his stepdaughter who was accusing him of molesting her child. Joe and I have known this man for some time and our hearts ached for the pain and confusion he was experiencing. I suggested that he put all of the people concerned on his stage and see a rainbow of lights around them. I encouraged him to release it to Divine Light and allow the greatest good for all concerned to manifest. I even promised him that if he did so, the entire business would be over within two weeks. He shook his head, wondering how that could be possible since the stepdaughter had called a lawyer, gone to the police and was taking him to court. Nevertheless, in less than two weeks, he returned to tell us the astounding news that after the police had investigated, they found her story did not hold up and all charges were dropped.

I gave this jewel of wisdom to another lady who was having trouble with her tenant. It was very nasty with threats of court and untrue accusations. Again, within two weeks and without warning, the woman simply moved out and all charges were dropped. Miracles do still happen and it begins within your mind and heart.

Everyone, including yourself, is trying to avoid pain and find happiness and peace. When you let go of anxiety and worry and trust your angel and God to take care of all your needs, you will be at peace. It is often your perception of life that causes you to enter the state of fear. It is your beliefs and opinions that can get you into trouble. Everyone wants to be loved, praised, encouraged and worthy of the good things in life. Everyone wants inner peace and serenity. Begin now to trust that you will find it.

To do this, study the language of angels. Angels only speak of love. "Love is patient; love is kind and envies no one. Love is never boastful, nor conceited, not rude; never selfish, not quick to take offense. There is nothing love cannot face; there is no limit to its faith, its hope, and its endurance. In a word, there are three things that last forever: faith, hope and love; but the greatest of them all is love."(1 Corinthians 13) Angels are patient, kind and certainly can't envy us poor humans. They are never boastful, nor conceited, never rude or selfish and never take offense even when we're at our worst. There is nothing we do that will turn our angel away from us. There is no limit to their faith in us even when we don't have faith in ourselves. They continue to hope for us to choose love even when we choose to wallow in fear. Their love will endure forever.

One way to discover your purpose *for the moment* is to listen to your heart's desires. What is it you would *really like to do, become, feel, experience?* Is your soul speaking? Do you believe your desires are possible? Why, or why not? Do you believe you are too old? Too poor? Too dumb? What? What keeps you from your goals?

Listen to your emotions. What excites you? What turns you on? If you could really do anything, go anywhere, be anyone. . .who or what would it be? How can you incorporate something of these feelings into your own life now?

Listen to your body. Do you have allergies? Do you have discomfort or pain? Look for a play on words as any part of your body speaks to you. Pay close attention to your body this week. Hear it. Let it speak the truth about who you are and why you're here.

Louise Hay has been teaching the truth about the body for quite some time. Her book, *You Can Heal Your Life,* gives positive affirmations for any illness you create. She believes that you are 100% responsible for all of your experiences because every thought is creating your future. I believe that as well. She says, "Whenever you are ill, you need to search your heart to see who it is you need to forgive. . .the very person you find it hardest to forgive is the one YOU NEED TO LET GO OF THE MOST. Forgiveness means giving up, letting go. It has nothing to do with condoning behavior. . .It's just letting the whole thing go. We do not have to know HOW to forgive. All you need to do is to be WILLING to forgive. The Universe will take care of the hows."

Forgiving can seem impossible to some people. During one reading, it was revealed to me the beauty of a woman's aura and the goodness that was within her. She soaked up this information and asked for more. Then, the angels revealed a deep-seated anger toward her sister and brother. Gently, her angel suggested that she forgive them. The change in the woman's aura was amazing. Red fired through it like sparks from a flame. She exclaimed that she would *never forgive them*. I held up my hand to calm her and said the forgiveness was not *for them, but for herself* in order to let go of the pain. She refused to discuss it further.

We concluded the reading by having her draw one of the forty angel cards that accompany the *Letters From Your Guardian Angel*, an inspired work given to me by my angels. It didn't surprise me that she drew Forgiveness. She took the letter and went on her way only to return moments later to throw the letter down on my table and exclaim, "Here, give this to some other fool." She stalked away, claiming she would never return to the Psychic Fair where I was giving mini readings with other psychics. After hundreds of readings, this was the first person who reacted to me and my angels in such an angry manner. Whenever I think of her, I send rainbows of healing light to surround her. Someday she will hear the voice of her own angel within, whispering, "Open your heart. . .and forgive."

You use that Ocean of Divine Energy to create whatever you choose. Once you realize that *you create your world by how you think and through what you believe*, you can change what you don't like. You can begin to feel like you have some control over your life. I have a teacher-friend of mine who keeps saying she wants to meet Mr. Right, but he's "hiding from her." If she could listen to herself, she'd begin to understand how she aborts any good she could create by the negative programming in her daily speech habits. It's like sending a message to your angel, saying, "I want to meet Mr. Right." And in the next breath you say, "But wait until I lose weight," or "Wait until you can come up with someone who's young, rich, tall, dark and attractive." After awhile, your angel just waits until you make up your mind about what you really want.

There is one other thing you need to understand about the creative process – of life, that is. Your soul has a say in what goes on in your life's drama. It has an agenda that may draw people and situations onto your stage. Your life story may not be how you might plan it. If you had your druthers, you'd be rich, beautiful/ handsome, talented, kind and wonderful. So how come you're not? (I assume you aren't or you wouldn't be reading this now!) You aren't because your life would not be any fun at all with no drama, challenges or sudden changes of plans. It's like playing a pinball machine that you could win all the time. What fun is that? Pretty boring after awhile.

Soul Mates

This is probably the most asked question in a reading, "When will I meet my soul mate?" I don't care what age a person is, they want to know who will be their partner in this dance of life. The idea of a soul mate comes with the pursuit of marital bliss and happiness. Most people believe they are not complete until they find a life-partner. It is this concept that gets most people in trouble.

The angels have shown me how relationships with a partner serve many purposes. As I mentioned above, it is a mirroring process that enables you to go within and discover who you really are. Unfortunately, it is more often from a "dysfunctional" relationship that we gain the most rather than from one that seems "perfect."

So often I am shown past lives that were intertwined in a conflict and are being resolved in some way in this lifetime. The "scales of justice" become balanced one way or another. If I sense a relationship is ending, I don't reveal it by bluntly saying, "I see you're getting a divorce sometime in the future." Instead, their angel will reveal the relationship with such clarity that the client can see it from a different perspective. Sometimes a past life will astutely describe a relationship *in reverse* of the present one, like the flipside of a coin. Since I have no idea who is who, I simply leave it up to the client to tell the rest of the story.

For example, I was shown a scenario where a 14th century woman had been abandoned by her husband who went off to war. He was killed, leaving her with three small children. The anger at being deserted was carried over into this lifetime where the "woman" now played the role of the husband. The woman who came for the reading was carrying over some heavy-duty guilt from abandoning her family in that 14th century lifetime. She explained how she bent over backwards to please her husband, who always seemed so angry with her. Although the marriage was not good, she was determined to make it work.

When her husband suddenly "abandoned" her with three small children, she was confused and hurt. She simply couldn't understand how he could do this when she worked so hard to please him. She felt devastated. When I explained the past life vision showed a "reverse karma" where she and her husband were playing the opposite roles to experience in full what had been inflicted in that 14th century life, she began to let go. I showed her how her angels were encouraging her to not only forgive him, but herself; the woman began to let go and move on with her life. The scales had been balanced.

If things are not going well in a relationship, is it always a balancing from a previous lifetime? No. There are a multitude of reasons for "good" and "bad" relationships or experience. When we simply let go and trust that we will be given the answers in God's perfect time, we will know.

Summary

Why are you here? The experiences of this physical dimension are filled with gems of wisdom that extend beyond many dimensions. Our soul chooses to learn how to create beauty, peace, love and joy through confusion, pain and fear.

Following are some words describing those paradoxes. I call it the "Pendulum of Opposites." When you can reconcile each experience by moving to a **neutral** position between positive and negative poles, you're in touch with your soul. Often, your electromagnetic field of energy swings back and forth between these two. The more you become neutral or grounded, the greater control you have over your life. Look at those people or incidents that "push your buttons." As soon as you become aware of them, take a deep breath and step aside. Allow the **law of nonresistance** to play here. Like the martial art of Karate, once you understand momentum of energy, you can control it. If someone comes rushing at you, either literally or with words, the force of their blow could be devastating. But if you were to step aside, the force of their momentum would cause them to fall flat. You learn to get out of life's way.

Pendulum of Opposites

Negative	Neutral	Positive
Addictive	Detached	Withdrawn
Aggressive	Content	Passive
Analyze	Trust	Synthesize
Anxious	Peaceful	Excited
Chaos	Order	Perfectionism
Competitive	Cooperative	Noncompetitive
Contemptible	Appreciative	Noble
Control	Accept	Release
Criticize	Encourage	Flatter
Death	Transition	Life
Deception	Openness	Naiveté
Depleted	Constant	Vibrant
Despair	Peace	Hope
Destroy	Oneness	Create
Dissonance	Peace	Harmony
Divide	Oneness	Unite
Doubt	Knowledge	Certainty

Empty..................	Complete..................	Full
Falsehood..................	Wisdom..................	Truth
Fear..................	Love..................	Joy
Guilt	Wisdom..................	Innocence
Hide..................	Know..................	Reveal
Ignorance..................	Wisdom..................	Knowledge
Rigid..................	Content..................	Relaxed
Sacrifice..................	Love..................	Service
Sad..................	Balanced..................	Happy
Self-deprecation..................	Unconditional Love..................	Self-love
Selfish..................	Compassionate..................	Generous
Separation..................	Oneness..................	Togetherness
Take..................	Be..................	Give
Tense..................	Content..................	Relaxed
Undecided..................	Know..................	Decisive
Impatience..................	Tolerance..................	Patience
Lack..................	Oneness..................	Abundance
Lust..................	Fulfillment..................	Desire
Reject..................	Know..................	Accept
Revenge..................	Balance..................	Forgive

Your guardian angel will come to you through a guided visualization on side three of the tapes that accompany this book. This will be a different representation of your angel. Be open to receive this gift. Let your playful imagination create the scene within your mind without judging or analyzing it. Let it flow and enjoy it. Feel free to speak with this Being of Light and ask it questions. Let it reveal your purpose.

Do not worry if you can't "see" clearly at first. It's quite different from watching television that uses your physical eyes. Rather, use your inner eye that imagines what something looks like. You get a sense or feeling of an image, a knowing more than a picture. For example, one lady said she couldn't see her angel but felt it had blond hair and blue eyes. That's perfect. Our imagination works through the sense of intuition or feeling. Trust whatever comes. Do not question it. Let it flow. The tape keeps the left side of your brain busy with words that draw images from the right side. Simply follow it and let yourself be.

Journal Entries for Week Three

Directions: Listen to side three of the tapes all this week. Record your images and impressions in your journal. Take one or two of the questions given below each day to observe and record in your journal. Read them through first at the beginning of the day and choose which one you will play with.

1. After listening to the tape, write as much detail about your guardian angel as you can remember.
2. Describe your "stage and orchestra." List those who needed tuning up. Each day as you listen to the tape, record your impressions. They will change each time.
3. When you are feeling rushed and harried, pause, take a deep breath and enter your Inner Sanctum. Picture your angel and feel its love and peace surrounding you.
4. Record any incidents of the day where you needed to be calm and serene.
5. Record any moments this week when you felt anger and impatience. Who "pushed your buttons?" What was that person's need? What need of yours was not fulfilled? How could you change your reactions to the situation should it occur again?
6. Make a list of all your strengths and abilities.
7. Make a list of all your fears of inadequacy, loss, lack, etc.
8. Make a list of the qualities of personality and character you would like to have. Start by listing the people you admire and look at what specifics you see in them that you would like to have as well.
9. Select one strength and one fear that you will highlight this week. Make a point of seeing how you can improve the quality of your life with the gifts you have been given.
10. Make a list of the people on your Inner Stage and practice daily releasing them to Divine Light and their guardian angel.

Chapter 4
Where Am I Going
And How Soon Will I Get There?

Do angels hop and skip and play,
Or do they sit and pray all day?
Do angels know their lessons well?
Do angels have "Show and Tell?" I wonder.

Do angels swing upon the stars?
Do they dance and play on Mars?
Do angels visit us on Earth?
Do they play and laugh and giggle in mirth? I wonder.

There is a driving need within most of us to understand who we are and why we're here. We want to know what life is all about. Why did this or that happen? We want to know where we're going and how quickly we'll get there. We want to know when we'll get that perfect job, perfect partner, perfect life. This chapter deals with that basic need that drives us to astrologers and psychics. We will try to view each of the forms of divination from an angelic perspective.

What is Astrology?
"Astrology is the science that explores the action of celestial bodies upon animate and inanimate objects, and their reactions to such influences. Astrology has its place among the earliest records of human learning. It is the parent of astronomy: for many years they were one science. Now, astronomy is a science of distances, magnitudes, masses, motions, speeds, locations, and so on, based upon observations made with instruments like the telescope. Astronomy may therefore be termed an 'objective' science, while as-

trology must be termed a 'subjective' science. Thus, the charting of the horoscope is really an astronomical process; the judgment of delineation of the horoscope is an astrological process.

"Astrology also deals with angles between the planets and their observed effect upon humanity. The signs are a way of dividing the heavens; so are the houses, but they are based upon the place of birth. The sign may be considered the field of action; the house is the place where the action occurs, and the planet is the motivating power or force.

"Astrology teaches us that there is harmony and symmetry in the universe and that everyone is part of the whole. Thus, you should try to understand astrology as a philosophy which helps to explain life, and not as a predictive art or science. The purpose of astrology is not to blame the planets for what happens to us, but, on the contrary, to learn about ourselves by planetary indication. When we see ourselves clearly we can discover within ourselves new qualities, and thus our lives can become more fulfilled, purposeful and productive." (*The Only Way to Learn Astrology, Volume One,* Astro-Analytic Publ., 1981.)

When people use astrology as a tool to learn more about themselves to grow in wisdom and live in love, they are using it the right way. When people use astrology to predict their future, they are acting out of fear of what might happen. They fear loss of control, believing that if they only knew "the bad" ahead of time, they could change it. In a way, they are right. Nothing is written in stone about the future. You do have free will and can change some things, but not the basic plan your soul has set up. Fear can create a dependency upon astrology, horoscopes and other forms of "fortune telling." It demonstrates a lack of trust in God, your angel or yourself.

Astrology has always intrigued me even though I don't know much about it. I had my "birth chart" done and was amazed at how accurately it described not only my personality, but my life. I once took a class in astrology, determined to sort out all the earth, fire, water and air signs. I made flash cards. I studied. But today, I don't even know whose sign is whose. It just didn't stick in my brain. "In one ear and right out the other" as they say. I came to the conclusion that my soul didn't want to learn astrology this time around. Perhaps it already has. Anyway, I guess they, (my soul and angels), want me to focus on helping people their way. They have revealed more to me about people through my simple form of "reading," than all the books in the world could teach me. For this I am grateful. Besides, I always was lazy.

Strongest Planetary Influences

Sun: Life-giving energy and growth, power urge, ego, inner self.

Moon: Tides in large bodies of water; water and emotions within the physical body.

Mercury: Communication.

Saturn: Karmic lessons, called the "Teacher," the need for security and safety.

Mars: Aggressive urge, initiative, energy.

Venus: Social urges, sense of value, affection.

Most teachers will agree that the full moon has an impact on their students' emotions. The increase in confrontations and even fights made us conclude that the moon affects everyone. It's also easy to observe the moon's cycles in the tides of the planet's large bodies of water as well as the cycles that involve the fluids within our own bodies. Is it so difficult to conclude that other planets may be causing some pull to our emotions or our lives in some way as well?

I like to compare astrology to the story of Sleeping Beauty. The stars are like your good fairies who arrive at your birth, sprinkling you with the star dust of individual planets that will give you physical beauty and wonderful personality characteristics. But there's always a bad fairy or two who will throw in some planets that will make life interesting and challenging. The fairy godmother is your guardian angel who helps to keep all those elements balanced by encouraging you to call upon your strengths and gifts to overcome challenges. For example, self doubt can keep you from becoming self-absorbed, but too much can cause depression. A temper can become an asset when you use it to recognize your needs and calmly define what is beneficial for your happiness. Likewise, stubbornness can be turned into perseverance when you get fear of embarrassment out of the way. There are twelve signs in the zodiac with a natural planetary ruler. This means that one planet will have a stronger influence on your life than others. This influence can be positive or negative depending on how you choose to view it.

Astrological Signs and Personal Characteristics
Aries, The Ram, March 21 – April 19

Positive qualities: pioneering, executive, competitive, impulsive, eager, courageous, independent, dynamic, lives in the present, quick.

Negative qualities: domineering, quick-tempered, violent, intolerant, hasty, arrogant, "me first" attitude, brusque, lacks follow-through.

Taurus, The Bull, April 20 – May 20

Positive: patient, conservative, domestic, sensual, thorough, stable, dependable, practical, artistic, loyal.

Negative: self-indulgent, stubborn, slow-moving, argumentative, short-tempered, possessive, greedy, materialistic.

Gemini, The Twins, May 21 – June 21

Positive: dual, congenial, curious, adaptable, expressive, quick-witted, literary, inventive, dexterous, clever.

Negative: changeable, ungrateful, scatterbrained, restless, scheming, lacks concentration and follow-through.

Cancer, The Crab, June 22 – July 22

Positive: tenacious, intuitive, maternal, domestic, sensitive, retentive, helpful, sympathetic, emotional, good.

Negative: brooding, touchy, too easily hurt, negative, manipulative, too cautious, lazy, selfish, tends to feel sorry for self.

Leo, The Lion, July 23 – August 23

Positive: dramatic, idealistic, proud, ambitious, creative, dignified, romantic, generous, self-assured, optimistic.

Negative: vain, status-conscious, childish, overbearing, fears ridicule, cruel, boastful, pretentious, autocratic.

Virgo, The Virgin, August 24 – September 22
Positive: industrious, studious, scientific, methodical, discriminating, fact-finding, exacting, clean, humane, perfectionist.
Negative: critical, petty, melancholy, self-centered, fears poverty and disease, picky, pedantic, skeptical, sloppy.

Libra, The Scales, September 23 – October 23
Positive: cooperative, persuasive, companionable, peace-loving, refined, judicial, artistic, diplomatic, sociable, suave.
Negative: fickle, apathetic, loves intrigue, peace at any price, pouting, indecisive, easily deterred.

Scorpio, The Scorpion, October 24 – November 22
Positive: motivated, penetrating, executive, resourceful, determined, scientific, investigative, probing, passionate, aware.
Negative: vengeful, temperamental, secretive, overbearing, violent, sarcastic, suspicious, jealous, intolerant.

Sagittarius, The Archer, November 23 – December 22
Positive: straightforward, philosophical, freedom-loving, broad-minded, athletic, generous, optimistic, just, religious, scholarly, enthusiastic.
Negative: argumentative, talkative, procrastinates, exaggerates, self-indulgent, blunt, impatient, gambler, pushy, hot-headed.

Capricorn, The Sea-goat, December 23 – January 19
Positive: cautious, responsible, scrupulous, conventional, businesslike, perfectionist, practical, hard working, economical, serious, traditional.
Negative: egoistic, domineering, unforgiving, fatalistic, mind rules heart, stubborn, brooding, inhibited, status-seeking.

Aquarius, The Water-bearer, January 20 – February 18
Positive: independent, inventive, tolerant, individualistic, progressive, artistic, scientific, logical, intellectual, altruistic.
Negative: unpredictable, temperamental, bored by detail, cold, fixed in opinions, shy, eccentric, radical, impersonal, rebellious.

Pisces, The Fish, February 19 – March 20
Positive: compassionate, charitable, sympathetic, emotional, sacrificing, intuitive, introspective, musical, artistic.
Negative: procrastinating, over-talkative, melancholy, pessimis-

tic, emotionally inhibited, timid, impractical, indolent, feels misunderstood.

Each sign is like a blueprint of a soul's life plan. It gives the personality talents to develop and challenges to overcome or turn into assets. You can tell how old a soul is by how well they have overcome the negative qualities of their sign and turned them into assets. Both positive and negative qualities are for spiritual gain through knowledge and wisdom. It is the person's choice as to how it will develop the tools that are given to sculpt the actions and reactions to each experience. It is *always* a choice between love and fear. When love is the motivating factor, "good" returns; when fear is the activator, "bad" returns. But your angel does not see "good" or "bad" as you do. It sees only experiences that bring knowledge and wisdom to the soul and an eventual awakening to the God Presence within.

Horoscopes

There are some people who never begin their day without first reading their horoscope in the newspaper. Just like the list above, a horoscope is much too general for it to clearly describe an individual. To have an accurate reading, the astrologer needs the place, date and time of your birth. For those people who don't know the time of their birth, their chart will not be as exact. Also the rising sign or planet that is found on the horizon of your chart will have a great influence over your personality. For example, I'm a Leo, but my rising sign is Libra which means that I have a need for harmony and fair play. My astrologer back in 1988 wrote, "You much cared for and nurtured children in this life and probably in your last. But now you come to do a whole new thing, something different to involve yourself in a whole new way of thinking, a revolutionary way of thinking. It is futuristic." Some people might term this book a whole new way of thinking!

Astrology is a complex system of understanding yourself. For those of you who are interested in this study, you will find it challenging and fascinating and well worthwhile.

Control Versus Influence

You have to remember that you *are not controlled by the stars or planets – only influenced by them.* They are the form from which your soul molded your body and personality. They are the stuff from which you experience that unexpected turn of events in life, (when Mercury goes retrograde and communication falls apart). Once, my friend Mary and I agreed to meet halfway at a restaurant on a specific day at a specific time. I got there early, went in, got a table and read a book while I waited. . .and waited. . .and waited. Finally, I went home. Later, I found out that Mary had been there, had come into the restaurant, looked around for me and then went outside and waited. . .and waited. . .and finally went home.

The angels just showed me a curious picture of sound waves bouncing erratically like static on a radio. Perhaps they're trying to say that's what happens when Mercury is retrograde. Our ability to hear and respond to one another or to our angel is dulled by this static. Interesting, isn't it? Like an electrical storm that turns out the lights, we just have to wait it out.

You come here with a set of tools that make up who you are. They can mold and change anything, even your body and personality with one of those tools: the use of your free will. There isn't any event or experience in itself that dictates who you are, but rather *it is how you choose to react to these unexpected actions* that creates your outer physical world.

If you could only conclude that **you are here to grow and learn for** *the joy of it,* you'd experience challenges as opportunities for obtaining new knowledge. Think about all the stories of heroes. Let's take a modern-day hero as an example. Mohammed Ali, who now has Parkinson's disease as a result of his boxing, was featured on the television show, *Sixty Minutes.* It was shown how he has grown into a generous and loving person *because of his disability and his religious beliefs.* From one who was called, "The Mouth," to one who can hardly speak, he took that challenge in his life and gained great knowledge and truth from it. It has also gained him the admiration and love of his many fans.

Free Will = Choices

Choice **is the key word here**. You may feel helpless in the unexpected events that occur in your life, but you **always have a choice as to how you will react to them**. You can rant and rave and beat yourself up, or you can accept what you cannot change and make the best of it. For example, let's suppose you had a flat tire in a remote area. You could cuss and fume and kick the tire. But sooner or later you'd have to change it and move on. The difference here is that if you react in rage to a situation you cannot change, *it changes your life.* You could probably go home and continue to rant and rave and kick the poor dog thus extending the reaction to the experience by creating more confusion in your life. Or. . .you could take a deep breath, give thanks to your soul and angel for the opportunity to practice joy. You could whistle a happy tune while changing the blasted tire.

It is always your choice. I know because I've had flat tires, too. Once it happened on a side street and as my car limped around the corner, there was a tire store! Honest. Every time I've had a flat tire, within minutes I've had help without lifting a finger. When you acquire the habit of reacting with a peaceful mind and heart, you create good rather than "bad." Notice I've said "acquire the habit." It takes a determined effort to exchange one habit for another. First you have to recognize it and then you have to deliberately *choose again.*

What is Numerology?

Numerology is like astrology in that it uses a complex system of defining the aspects of one's life. Some say it is even older than astrology, while others say they are branches of the same thing. Numerology takes a person's name at birth and the date of birth as the basis for the information. It changes the letters into numbers and adds them together. It always reduces any double-digit number down to a single digit by adding them together.

For example the letter A is 1; B is 2 and so on. But it is not our purpose here to give you a lesson on numerology, but to acquaint you with another interesting way of gaining insights into who you really are. Numerology has drawn my interest much more than astrology, but I'm not even an amateur in either one. The basic meaning of the numbers makes sense to me and I often apply them to my everyday life to increase my awareness and understanding.

When I had a chart done, it described my personality quite accurately; but when it said I would marry a foreigner, I dismissed it. I was already married to an Irishman, so I figured it had to be wrong. Little did I know that many years in the future, I would be married to Joe Calleja who is from the island of Malta, south of Sicily.

Below is a brief summary of the "vibrations" or qualities of each of the numbers as they relate to the events of our lives:

One means a "new beginning" or a start of a new project. It means individuality and initiative, a restlessness, a craving for new ideas and new experiences.

Two means partnerships, companionship, decisions or choices to be made between two things, peace and compromise.

Three refers to creativity such as 2 + 1 = 3, or a man and a woman creating a child. It refers to activity which might mean the creation of a project, or travel, or simply the joy of living. Some say things happen in three's like past, present and future; the primary colors of red, yellow and blue; the three-dimensional world of length, breadth and width and so on. Expansion, growth and creativity as a result of the mind, our soul and our angel coming together.

Four is more stable like the four legs of a chair. It refers to law and order, to career or work or simply all the material things of life. It refers to form built as a result of merger and expansion.

Five centers on communication, decisions and change with its restless energy that keeps you on the move. It brings experience needed to deal with the new world of form.

Six brings harmony, peace and beauty with emphasis usually on home and family. It can mean partnerships, marriage, love and balance, resulting from the experience of five.

Seven is symbolic of rest and perfection. It refers to physical completion and health as well as a time for turning inward and expanding spiritually. It is often referred to as a heavenly number, the day of rest after God created the universe.

Eight centers around the law of "Cause and Effect" or "Karma" which means simply, "What goes around comes around," or "You will reap what you sow." It refers to responsibility for the actions you choose. The number eight is symbolic of infinity and means balance and strength.

Nine is the last number and denotes endings and/or transitions which lead to wisdom. It is a time of summing up, evaluating and letting go of old ideas, of no longer needed material possessions and outdated relationships.

Just for fun, I like to add up the numbers in my address, phone number or license plate and see what it has to say to me. Sometimes I check out the numbers on the digital clock as I glance at it. Once I kept seeing 11:11 on the clock – often twice a day! This went on for almost a year. It was uncanny. When I would try to catch it, I couldn't. Then I ran across an article that explained 11/11 to mean the opening of a portal to greater spiritual awareness. It was at a time of my life when my career as a psychic went "public" and many more people became aware of it. Another time, I kept seeing 5:55 on the clock. I took that to mean big changes were coming but with ease and harmony because 5+5+5 =15 and 1 + 5 = 6 or harmony. At that time, Joe and I had decided to turn our home into a mini-retreat center and began a five-year project of renovation. There was that "five" again!

The Cycles of Life

The angels tell me it is important for people to understand the cycles of life. We've already discussed moon cycles and how they affect our bodies. Study of astrology can tell you how your personality may react during any given cycle. I felt it would be helpful for you to have an overview of different cycles and how they may affect your life. They are a combination of astrology and numerology and will help you understand the ebb and flow of your life. You can learn when to move forward and when to hold back.

Fifty-two Day Cycle

This first type of cycle is explained by Joseph Weed in *Wisdom of the Mystic Masters*, (Parker Pub., 1968). He gives the best times to begin a business or project, periods to watch your health and many other helpful suggestions. For example, he explains that life has its ups and downs and can be understood through close examination of the cycles of life. To determine your cycles, begin with your birthday and count 52 days for cycle one, then count that same day as number one of cycle two and so on. Following is a brief summary for each period:

Life Cycle, First Period: This is a time to ask for favors, to seek employment or loans or business concessions, to form partnerships or to make investments. This is also a good time to advance yourself among the people of your city, state or country, to build up your credit standing or your reputation. This is the best time for you to push yourself forward with determination so far as your name, your integrity and your honor are concerned.

Life Cycle, Second Period: This period is distinctly different from the first. Best for short journeys or trips of immediate importance and for changes that can be started and finished within the period itself. Not good for a change of business, the start of a new career or making any permanent change such as contracts, lending or borrowing money. Not good for starting construction or beginning a project that requires substantial investment. Not good to speculate in the stock market or to gamble in any form.

Life Cycle, Third Period: In this cycle, exercise good judgment. With a great inflow of energy, you may want to do great and important things. If directed carefully, it can be the best time to improve your health, build up your business or anything that requires a great deal of energy – you have it now. But don't overdo. You may be tempted to bite off more than you can chew! It's a good time to finish things you didn't have energy for previously.

Life Cycle, Fourth Period: Mental and spiritual natures are stimulated; an excellent time for writing books, producing plays or making plans requiring imagination and quick thinking and the ability to express thoughts lucidly. New ideas will come rapidly;

grasp them before they're forgotten. Act on impulses and hunches. You will be optimistic but somewhat nervous and restless. Good time to deal with literary people, writers, journalists, book or magazine publishers, but be careful to scrutinize all legal and other documents because deception is possible and it is a period when falsehood is as eloquently and easily expressed as the truth. Study and gain information and knowledge, but not a good time to get married, hire help or buy a house or property.

Life Cycle, Fifth Period: This is a time for you to achieve greater success in your personal affairs. Your interest will expand and your prosperity increase. Your mind will become sharper and clearer; relationships become more open as you gain confidence. This is the best period for dealing with the law or people of prominence. Good to begin new ventures that may take some time or to take long journeys. Good time for stock, but nothing that is not completely legitimate!

Life Cycle, Sixth Period: This is the best time for rest, relaxation and amusement. Business will continue to prosper, but now is the time to take trips to renew old friendships or make new friends. Good for business matters that touch upon art, music, literature, sculpture, etc. It is a good period for a man to seek favors or business agreements from a woman, just as the third period is better for women to obtain favors from men. Best period to buy stocks or bonds for investment and to employ others.

Life Cycle, Seventh Period: This is the most critical period of your yearly cycle. During this 52-day period, it's time for housecleaning, for making room for the new and better. This may cause distress and a sense of loss and may tempt you to foolish actions and decisions. It is a period of endings to open to a period of beginnings and new opportunities.

Personal Year Cycle

The following system of cycles spans nine years before it repeats itself. It describes the pull toward action in a defined direction. These cycles are found in Dusty Bunker's book, *Dream Cycles*.

You determine your "Personal Year Cycle" by your birthdate

– month and day only, (not the year). Translate the month into numbers and add them individually to the day. For example if your birthday is November 15th, (11/15), you would add $1 + 1 + 1 + 5 = 8$. If your birthday was January 19th, (1/19), you would add $1 + 1 + 9 = 11$ and then add those together to equal 2.

To this number add the year **of your last birthday.** For example, if your birthday is 11/15, you came up with the number 8. If this is say, August, 1996, you would not have had a birthday yet so you would add 8 to 1995 like this: $8 + 1 + 9 + 9 + 5 = 32$ which you again add together: $3 + 2 = 5$. You would be in your Fifth Year Cycle. The following is a summary of those cycles that may give you greater knowledge about yourself.

Year One – Key words: new beginnings, action, change, new ideas, making decisions on your own without help from others. This is a year to begin new projects, new relationships, new friends. It brings change into your life. You will experience a sense of isolation. Even if you seek help from another, it most likely won't be what you're looking for, so you'll dismiss it. Concentrate on figuring out who you are, go within and pay attention to your thoughts and feelings. Don't be afraid to express yourself and your needs in this year. This is your "wish year." Make a list of all the things you want to accomplish and strive to obtain them. They say, "Be careful what you wish for. It may come true." In this year, that possibility is greatest. Now is your time.

Be on guard against overindulgence in this year cycle. Loving oneself does not mean abusing the body with run-a-way appetites or self-gratification. In this year, you may find an abundance of energy. Use it wisely. Don't waste it in too many physical pleasures. Use it to gain spiritual growth through additional knowledge about yourself and the world around you.

Year Two – Key words: harmony, balance, patience, co-operation, mediation, passivity. This is a time to be a magnet for what you need and desire. Wait for it to come to you. This is the exact opposite of the previous year where you went out to get what you wanted. Now is the time to watch those efforts pay off and be returned to you. Of course, if you wasted the year, there won't be anything to wait for now. If you did plant some seeds of growth, go within and nurture that seed with quiet meditation and patience. Yet, this is not a dull year by any means. Expect the unexpected. You may have to make quick decisions that require discrimination and good judgment. Examine the fine print in any contracts or agreements to avoid deception. Buying and selling are strong possibilities in this year. Love and marriage are also possible. Be open to others with a loving and sharing heart.

You may find yourself center stage this year with recognition for your efforts and creative abilities. You will be motivated to express your talents in new and innovative ways. Yet, this is not a year to push ahead. Wait, because you may be too sensitive or emotional this year to have the best perspective. Try not to take things too seriously. Watch out for the temptation to "accept peace at any price." Strive for balance and inner peace. That means going within and taking time to meditate. Bunker suggests, "A disruption of the two cycle of attraction and harmony can bring separation." This is likely because you may tend to be overly sensitive.

Year Three – Key words: scattering, freedom, entertainment, self-expression. This is a time of growth and expansion, a time to improve yourself because hope and optimism abound. Happiness is the keynote for you this year. You may decide to travel on long trips, or you may have the desire to entertain. This may stimulate you to choose a new look for yourself with a new hairstyle or makeover. You may find youself the life of the party as your self-expression peaks in this cycle. Share your talents with others. Lucky money may come your way, but don't go spending a fortune on the lottery! What we often fail to remember is that previous actions bring fruit. A compulsion to overspend will be strong, so reign in the purse strings and be moderate in all things. This applies to your energies as well which may tend to feel scattered as you seek to do a hundred things at once. Be careful what you say about others. It will come back to you later and you may regret it.

Year Four – Key words: practicality, work, order, building foundations. This a year to focus on work. If you belong to an organization, you will become more active in it. This is a time for firming up the body that expanded in year three. It is the year of firming up the budget, cleaning out the closets and reorganizing your whole life. You will be motivated to start first in your home and then in your workplace.

This compulsion to organize is symbolic of the need to look within and reevaluate your beliefs and mindsets. It is a time to clean house mentally, emotionally and spiritually as well. Pay attention to where your eyes focus for reorganization. If it's the kitchen, look at your eating habits. If it's the bathroom, begin to release anger and expectations of others.

Because four is a solid number numerologically, it relates to your physical, material world. You may feel the need for security, for that comfort zone by surrounding yourself with "nice things." Money may become an issue now and your focus may reap rewards for you in direct proportion to the amount of effort you put into it. In year three, it was lucky money. Now it's earned "by the sweat of your brow." This may also be a time when a relationship with the opposite sex can be rewarding. Your body is highly tuned to the physical and its sensual enjoyment.

Year Five – Key words: change, freedom, new intellectual interests, travel, communication, sexual attraction, learning. This is a time when you seem to be too busy to think. You feel caught up in one event and activity after another. There are phone calls, meetings, short trips, invitations to mail and answer. It is a focus on communication and sometimes it will get mixed up because you're too busy to keep track! This is a time that you're sexually attractive, making it a good year for a mate to be drawn into your life. Avoid overdoing medications – even the over-the-counter type. Instead take time to do the breathing exercises in Chapter One to calm you and slow you down during this period and to help relieve the restless feelings that dominate. Remember to slow down to avoid accidents. This is a time when change comes quickly, but not through illness or accidents, please!

This is also a learning year. Take a class. Read books for knowledge as well as entertainment. Again, balance is important as always. You may be drawn to the color blue this year. This is the color of communication not just on the physical level, but also on the angelic level. Be prepared to make contact with your soul and your angel.

Year Six – Key words: family, health, service, listening to others' problems. Suddenly you become mother/father/sister/ brother to everyone you know. People will come to cry on your shoulders which will be broad enough for them. You become the home body who wants to redecorate, remodel or even sell your home and buy another. This is a time when your artistic inclinations blossom. Give them precedence in your time schedule, even if you don't believe you have time. Your soul is asking you to listen. What you learn in this cycle will carry over into another that will need the skills you develop now. This may be a time of graduations to attend, family weddings to go to, new babies, children leaving home. Again, the focus is on family and home.

Year Seven – Key words: self-analysis, achievement, health problems, rest, quiet meditation. This is the cycle that activates the mind and enables you to grow intellectually. Take a class, learn a new hobby, join a study group. It is a time to learn new things, to increase your talents to the next level. It is also a time to increase your own psychic abilities and spiritual growth. The number seven has long been considered a highly spiritual number. Take advantage of this time to really go within and listen. New ideas and wisdom will be given to you.

This is a good time to take a mini-vacation where nature can work its wonders on your body and mind. Concentrate on what's good about your life and let go of any concerns or issues. They will resolve themselves when you let your angel and soul take care of the details. Now is the time to release old anxieties. Consider this a period of incubation while the caterpillar rests inside the cocoon, waiting for the time that it can test its wings and fly. Rest and be at peace now.

Year Eight – Key words: business, power, responsibility, money, discipline, pressure, balance of relationships. This is the time to tighten the purse strings and buckle in for a budget overhaul. You will feel the flow of money has dried up and could become obsessive about it. This is simply an opportunity for you to let go and trust in your angel. What you have sown in the previous seven years will now be brought forth. If you've been self-indulgent and lax, you'll feel it now. If you've been diligent and disciplined, you'll reap the rewards. It is always this way.

This is also a time when you will receive recognition for your hard work, for projects successfully completed – again, the law of cause and effect making itself known to you. Intense relationships will force you to look at equal partnerships with respect for each person as separate individuals with a Divine Plan for their lives. It's a time to let go of expectations and mindsets about people around you. Let them be the best they can be without your interference. If you have worked at self improvement in the previous seven years, this one will be most rewarding.

Year Nine – Key words: giving to others, endings, service, transition. Again, it is time to clean house on all levels: physically, mentally, emotionally and spiritually. Sort out and let go of the things, (and people), that are no longer contributing to your greatest good. Let go of those comfort zones that keep you prisoner to the status quo that no longer serve your needs. But do not depend on your own conscious mind to make any major changes or decisions. We cannot see the whole picture. Our angel and soul can. Go within and ask for help in this "housecleaning."

Obvious and dramatic outer changes often take place now. People leave, like children going off to college or to get married. There may be job changes or moves to new locations. This will necessitate adjustments. It requires an ability to let go and move in the direction of the current of life that your soul has chosen. To swim against it will only cause discomfort. These changes are always for your greater good. You will know this when you finish this year and begin a new cycle next year.

You will find that many of your goals are reached. You will complete others that are still ongoing. The idea here is to finish the cycle and prepare for a brand new one without old stuff hanging on. Therefore, it is not a time to begin new projects. They would best wait until next year when your new cycle will nourish it and make it successful. This is an emotionally high time for you and again balance is the key. Really pay attention to the exercises in Chapter One that enable you to relax and go within. This is also a time to share your talents and resources with others. Charity is very much a part of this cycle. It's a way of giving back to the universe all that has been given to you in the past eight years. If you have given freely, with no strings attached, you will now be given in like kind. People will seem to go out of their way to do for you. On the other hand, if you have held on to people and things out of fear of loss, you may lose them during this year. You always reap what you sow. It's a universal law that no one can escape.

What is Psychometry?

Psychometry is another way of learning about oneself and others. It uses metal objects like jewelry that are worn daily to "pick up on" the vibrations of another person. The reader holds the object and is given feelings, ideas or images that describe the owner's life. This is the way I began reading others. At first, I thought it was my vivid imagination; but when people said it was accurate, I had to look again.

Seeing what one does not know creates believing. I had just met a new friend at a class and while driving her home, we talked about my new-found talent in psychometry. At her request to "experiment on her," I held her watch. For a few moments nothing came to me. Then I saw a large open book with Dorothy, (that's her real name and she said I could use it since she's now in spirit), turning the pages backwards. I saw a cluttered room with an enclosed stairway leading down. Dorothy exclaimed that just the day before she had been upstairs in her attic looking through an old photo album. And yes, there was an enclosed stairway leading down to the living room. Since I had never been in her home before it was doubly astounding to both of us. I became a believer in psychometry and my own budding psychic abilities. Dorothy became one of my greatest advocates and encouraged me when I had my bouts with self-doubt. Thank you, Dorothy!

Psychometry is also interesting when one tries to pick up on artifacts. It is said that no matter how old an item may be, it will hold the vibrations of its various owners. I can imagine how some items could tell quite a story.

What is Card Reading?

Tarot cards are often used to predict a person's future. They can be extremely accurate but often misunderstood, causing many to say that the cards are "tools of the devil." In my experience working with other psychics, I've come to appreciate their concern. When a reader is fearful and negative, their interpretation of the cards will reflect this. One reader said my husband, Joe, would either leave me or pass on within two to three months of the reading. She saw the "Destiny Card" and said there was nothing I could do to change it. When I said I did not accept that, she said the cards don't lie, but did act puzzled over the fact that there was no "Death Card" which is why she assumed he would simply "walk out."

I felt alarmed and angry at such a blatant interpretation that left no room for doubt. Of course she was wrong. Joe and I are still happily together years later and still devoted to one another. What she didn't even consider was the question I had asked the tarot as I shuffled the deck. The spread was supposed to answer that question. I had asked *What is my destiny with this present group of psychics.* I had been working with about ten people at what began as "Angel Fairs" and then became "Psychic Fairs." I hadn't felt really comfortable with them partly because of the negativity and the sense of competition among them with the focus on making money. That reading demonstrated the epitome of my concern and convinced me that the tarot was indeed right in its suggestion. *In two months,* I was going to begin the new year with the group. I interpreted the cards to be telling me that *I could walk out!* I think I stayed just to prove that I had free choice as everyone does. I also stayed to continue to be of service to the many clients who had come to me through the fairs and to work for the greater good of all the psychics within the group. I am happy to say as I write this that the group is now one of the best in Michigan, thanks to a dedicated leader who works hard to present us in a positive light.

What are Clairvoyants, Clairaudients and Channelers?

A clairvoyant is one who sees intuitively. I am considered a clairvoyant and visionary because I see pictures of a person's life that tell me how to best be of service to them. Since I ask the angels to help me in each session, I believe they are instrumental in giving me accuracy. They also give me the angelic viewpoint that reveals the soul's purpose for their life. This may include a past life revelation as it relates to people and circumstances surrounding the person in the present life.

A clairaudient is one who hears the words of an entity in spirit. Readers often speak of help from "guides" who are usually people who have passed over into the dimension of spirit and come to assist them. My own experience has proven this to be true. People who pass over stay pretty much the same. Some guides are very good and some are not.

The humorous movie, *Ghost*, depicts Whoopie Goldberg as a clairaudient psychic. She "heard" a spirit who had been murdered and desperately needed to warn his girlfriend that she was in danger. This movie depicted facts about the spirit world as well as fiction. Good psychics can hear those who pass on and will reveal information they could not possibly know.

Channeling is a means of allowing a spirit to speak through a physical entity. There are Christians who "speak in tongues." This is a form of channeling. Edgar Cayce was called "The Sleeping Prophet" because of his trancelike state when he channeled a healer of extraordinary abilities in the early forties. There are different levels of trance from light to deep states. Other channeled works I have come to respect are the "Michael" teachings that explore an elaborate system of the evolution of souls and the gentle humor of the "Emmanuel" books that encourage us to let go of fear and become the joyful beings of light that we are. We've already quoted Emmanuel and we'll discuss Michael later.

What are Psychics?

Let me clarify the meaning of the word "psychic." There is so much negative press about the word today that some people have become fearful of having anything to do with them. According to the dictionary, the word *psychic* relates to the power of the mind and the mental processes. It refers to the use of your mind beyond the limited 10% that most people use. It refers to the use of extrasensory perception and mental telepathy. The word comes from the Greek word hikos, "of the soul" and from psukhe, meaning "soul." So, as it is used here, we speak of becoming aware of your soul and your guardian angel. If you will stretch your mind to use more than that limited 10%, you will be able to play with the angels and dance for joy.

After a seminar, one of the participants exclaimed to a friend of mine that "Betty Rae is a normal person!" She was surprised that the other people attending were also. While some psychics may like to dress flamboyantly or put on a "Gypsy" costume, most of us are quite normal people who dress in business suits like the dignified old retired teacher that I am.

Most psychics have learned to tune in to their guides and angels for a greater view of the world and the people in it. They use the Alpha brain wave level of mind where they can see from a wider perspective than the conscious mind allows. Everyone has psychic abilities. Some call it "hunches" or "gut level feelings." Some just "know" that this or that is going to happen. And if it involves something "bad," they become fearful of this "gift." What they don't understand is that their own perspective is what colors what they "know." All the guides and angels cannot reveal anything to you except *through your mind and heart*. Remember, you are like that computer that has been programmed to read the world through your past experiences. Your guides can give you information that you didn't know before, but you must *process it through your data bank* of opinions and beliefs. You interpret what you are given from your unique viewpoint.

As with any talent – musical, artistic, *or* psychic – it requires a great deal of practice and determination in order to be proficient in it. It would be wise also to check a reader's attitude toward life. Are they positive and joyful, or fearful and pensive? Do they insist that what they know is correct? If so, beware. No one is 100% correct. Some say that even the best psychics are only 80% right. Pay attention to their main motivation for doing readings. Are they more concerned with how much money they will make rather than how they can be of service to you? Their interpretations will reflect this as well. In other words, if their focus is on the physical with its material gain and gratification, their way of looking at your reading will be on that level rather than on a spiritual level. But most people are interested in the everyday physical reality, so psychics give what is asked.

For example, on impulse, Joe and I went to a psychic in Texas. She read us both, but then asked that I leave the room. She then told Joe that there was a woman who was putting a hex on him out of revenge. Joe was puzzled, trying to figure out who this might be, but could not think of anyone who would try to do him harm. The psychic went on to explain that she could remove the hex for an additional amount of money. Joe gently but firmly declined. We quickly got out of there. It's sad that some people prey on the fears of others. This psychic didn't recognize that I was also psychic, or perhaps she would have "seen" differently.

It would be an illusion to describe a "good psychic" as one who refines a natural gift only for the greater honor and glory of God. Only saints are motivated to do that. We all desire appreciation and praise, and some seek their own honor and glory – and fame and fortune. But anyone who develops their natural psychic abilities to gain knowledge and wisdom about themselves or to be of service to others can gain a great deal of soul growth in one lifetime. Yet, God does not judge any of us. Nor can we judge others. But we can be discerning of the people with whom we trust to interpret the messages from our guides and angels. With this in mind, when you have a reading, take into your heart and soul what is said. Chew on it awhile. Digest the wisdom given from it. And then spit out the rest.

This book encourages you to unlock your own gifts by letting go of fear and doubt. My daughter's friend has a beautiful clairvoyant talent, but she often stifles it because of fear. Sometimes she can "see bad things happen to people" and believes that her gift is too much of a burden to bear. What she doesn't understand is that her definition of "bad" is out of fear and lack of knowledge. There is nothing in this world that cannot be turned into something for our greater good. It is only a matter of perspective.

There is a law of "noninterference" that some psychics ignore. They spout off their abilities like a child saying, "See what I can do." Let's suppose you have an intuition about someone becoming ill, or even dying, should you tell them about it? The answer is no. Not unless they ask you for a reading and it is revealed to you then. We have no right to interfere in another person's life. Yet, as with any rule, there are exceptions. If you *know* that someone's life is in danger, and you can do something about it, do it. If the person does not heed your warning, then let them be. Many psychics, including the well-known Jean Dixon, tried to warn John Kennedy of impending danger surrounding his trip to Texas, but he chose to ignore them. Each soul is playing out the game of life according to a plan. We cannot interrupt that plan simply because we were shown a glimpse of it. . .unless we are given the knowledge of what to do about it. The future is not carved in stone as some would have us believe.

An example of interfering came while I was preparing to read at a charity Psychic Fair. Before the event, a reader that I did not know handed me a photo face down. He asked me what I could get from it. Before I could comment another psychic stepped up and said, "He's dead and lying in a field somewhere." I was appalled. I could not believe that this woman could be so cruel, or that she would give information where it was not asked. I chose to ignore her and concentrated on the photo. I felt that it was a little animal whose picture I was holding. I described the animal's spirit that was right there with us and said that he would soon be present again in the next dog they purchased. I told him not to grieve for his pet for it would let him know of its presence. The woman psychic was right, but her presentation lacked a great deal. Unfortunately, there are a few psychics who have a need to show off!

Any reader who is dogmatic about the interpretation of information given may be unsure of his own abilities. No human being knows everything. In fact, no guide, higher self or even angel knows everything. Only God does. This is why we do not take anything given as absolute truth. After we take it into our inner tabernacle and test it out with our soul and angel, we can decide to keep it or ignore it. One mentor I studied with commented that she was not always right, but her guides were. I don't even accept that. *I know I'm fallible.* I know I can misinterpret some vision or symbol given. I also know the more I practice, the better I become. And I can tell that by the feedback I receive from my clients. Yet, fear and doubt block what you receive. Trust you will know what it is you need to know and open your heart to your guardian angel.

Let me stress that the majority of psychic readers seek to be of service to humankind. They try to uplift and inspire, to help each person reach their greatest potential. It is a sad thing when some are condemned simply because they ask for a fee for their services. We think nothing of paying a laborer for his time, or a lawyer or doctor. We pay our ministers, rabbis and priests. The spiritual people who work as psychics, mystics, clairvoyants, readers and visionaries are entitled to make a living as well. Intuitive people wrestle with their conscience about this and would rather not charge for spiritual work. They listen to others who try to tell them, "You will lose your gift if you charge money for it." That resonates fear, loud and clear. I do not accept fear. I do accept a donation for my time. The information from the angels is free. But, as in all professions, some are considered to be overpaid. Again, that is a judgment that only God and the individual can decide.

I remember the time when school teachers were expected to give of their knowledge and talent with very little recompense. When I began teaching in 1956, I received $3,600 annually. Todd received $3,800 to do the same thing – teach. I continued to study many years to obtain my Master's Degree. I had to pass tests and write a thesis. I kept going to school every year to learn more. I worked many hours outside of school to prepare my lessons and do the best I could for my students. Yet, many people believed I was paid too much; that I should give my time as a service to the community.

Just as some people will try to get information from a doctor without paying, so too, do people try to get free readings. Most people believe that this "gift" dropped on us out of the blue. Every reader I know worked hard to develop their natural intuitive powers through training, workshops, study and experience. The information I am giving to help you develop your own intuitive gifts will not come from simply reading this book. You first had to pay for the knowledge by buying the book, but it is up to you to put that knowledge into action through practice. I remember one person who called and asked if it was all right for them to copy my six-week class "Play Book" from a friend so she could take my class. I said, "No, it's copyrighted. It costs very little as part of the whole course." The person was indignant and did not take the class. Astounding how some people think.

It saddens me that my clients at the Psychic Fairs have to sign a waiver relieving me of responsibility for any action they may take from the information given. The waiver usually says something like, "This is for entertainment purposes only." Although I enjoy my work as an intuitive, and find great pleasure in it, I take it seriously. I do not like to be the "entertainment" at someone's party, unless I'm giving the party – an "Angel Party." In these group gatherings, I do keep it light, bringing my own board game and angel cards for people to use while I am giving short readings to individuals.

Some people think I can read their thoughts and may become uncomfortable when I'm nearby. I reassure them that I have learned to discipline my mind to close down until I am asked for help. I tell them it would be unethical for me to "read" them without their permission. It would be like a "Peeping Tom." And when people ask me to use my hard-earned intuitive powers to answer trivial questions in ordinary conversation, I tell them I do not do that. I explain that when I give a reading, I prepare myself for it through prayer and meditation. I explain that first I obtain permission from the client to do the reading and then ask God's permission as well. In that way, I am confident that whatever is given to me should be given to the client without holding anything back. I know that our angels see a bigger picture, and I've come to trust that.

On the other hand, one cannot get anxious about their work as a psychic, or take it too seriously. One lady commented that I was the first reader she had been to who actually joked and laughed in a reading. I was astounded. There is such joy and unconditional love that comes through from the angels. I cannot imagine not laughing when they give me a funny metaphor. Angels are *light* beings!

You may not wish to use your newly learned intuitive knowledge as a counselor like I have. But you can enrich your life by increasing your own awareness. You can gain the knowledge you need to solve problems and make decisions. I would love to be put out of business because you are listening to your own psychic within! One friend of mine has a gift for sensing when someone is pregnant. She's been right so often, it amazes her. But she wonders why she has this talent. "What good is it?" she asks. The good is in her becoming aware of her own abilities.

Summary

There are many more forms of self discovery that we have not included here. For example, a pendulum made of a weight on a string or chain can reveal your inner self or soul through simple yes or no questions. Palmistry studies the lines in your hands to tell a great deal about your personality and life. Another form of self revelation is your handwriting. It is a fascinating science that is used by law enforcement agencies to learn about people in crimes.

There are many inspirational card decks that uplift and give insight into your daily life. One of my favorites is called *The Inner Child Cards: A Journey into Fairy Tales, Myth & Nature* by Isha Lerner and Mark Lerner. I've always been fascinated by fairy tales and this one touches my heart. Their wisdom resonates with the wisdom that I've received from my angels. I often have a client pick a card after a reading and am amazed how it reflects what has been given from their angel.

You have many things to think about. Some of it may sing within your heart like music, while some may not. Take what you can and release the rest to the dusty bookshelves of the subconscious mind. I would suggest you toss it, but the mind doesn't throw anything away. The conscious mind creates the filing system. It sorts, evaluates, labels and puts ideas and things in order so it can learn and grow. With the help of your super-conscious mind, your soul, you can better evaluate all the incoming information. Your angel continues to encourage you to keep an open mind and not judge anything until you have all the facts.

Journal Entries for Week Four

Directions: Listen to side four of the tapes all this week. Write your impressions each time as they will change. Choose one or two of the following to write about in your journal each day.

1. List your talents and special gifts. No false modesty here. Write down the things that you have done about which you are most proud. What is your greatest achievement? Your angel will help you remember. Use the information given on the astrological signs from page 75. On a sheet of paper make three columns. At the top of column two put, "Assets." At the top of column three put "Challenges." In the first column write "Personality" and list your assets and weaknesses. Continue with the following items in column one: Physical, Financial, Material, Relationships, Occupation, Education: Knowledge/Information, Spiritual/Beliefs and any others that will help you become better acquainted with the Real You.

2. List things you would like to experience in this lifetime. Be reasonable but ambitious.

3. If your best friend were to describe you to a stranger, what would he/she say about you?

4. Carry on a conversation with your guardian angel and ask it to describe how it sees you. Remember, angels encourage and uplift. They never criticize or judge. They demonstrate God's unconditional love. Feel that Love surrounding you, enfolding you and flowing freely within you.

5. One day this week pay attention to what you think and say. There is a law of the Universe that says, "What you focus on expands." Ask your friends if they notice any negativity, judgment, criticism or self-condemnation coming from you. Ask them to be gentle!

6. One day this week, make it a point to say something kind to someone each day. Do something nice without anyone knowing it. Smile at all the people that you see.

7. One day this week observe people more closely. Watch their mannerisms, dress and speech. "Tune in" and see how many things you can remember about what you observed. Keep your journal handy to jot down your "hits" and "misses." When you watch a television drama, try to predict what someone will say or do.

8. This week when the phone rings, take a deep breath, go to your Inner Sanctum and imagine who is calling before you pick up the receiver.

9. In any new place, observe the room for a few seconds and then close your eyes and see how many objects you can name. After ascending or descending a flight of steps, recall how many there were.

10. Obtain an astrological reading from a reputable astrologer. Study your strengths and challenges. Discuss it with someone who knows you well.

11. List the magazines and newspapers you subscribe to. Put them under five categories: Spiritual, Physical, Intellectual, Emotional, Mixed. For example, *Time* magazine would be considered a mixture because it gives intellectual information, tells emotional stories and relates to the physical through sports. Which part do you read first? What does this say about you?

12. Describe a typical shopping day. What are your favorite shops? How much money do you spend on clothes? What brands do you buy? Examine your spending habits to learn more about the inner you.

13. List your favorite television shows under the categories: Spiritual, Intellectual, Emotional, Physical and Mixed. Does this

express a balance or do you tend to favor one over the others?

14. What do you consider entertainment? How often do you rest and relax? How often do you treat yourself to a night out?

15. Have you ever felt the need to "get into shape?" What motivated you to feel that way and what did you do about it?

16. How many classes, seminars or new things have you learned this past year?

17. List the books you have read under the five categories: Spiritual, Intellectual, Emotional, Physical and Mixed. For example, a romance novel would be listed under "Emotional."

18. How much time do you give to prayer and meditation? To physical exercise? To career/work? To play? To rest and sleep?

19. Total up your answers to see how much time and thought you give to the four aspects of who you really are: Spirit, Mind, Emotions and Body Physical. Are you in balance, or do you tend to lean more to one than the others?

Chapter 5
There's Never Enough Time!

Frolicking angels come dancing and singing
To rescue us from time and space.
They lift us up above noise and chaos.
They bring us peace. They slow our pace.

Fluttering angels come laughing and playing,
Calling to you and me.
They whisper to us, "Don't be afraid.
We'll teach you joy; we'll set you free."

The Illusion of Time

In this physical world, we experience the illusion of time and space. Time is a reality only in the mind – not in the real world of spirit. When I'm giving a reading, I am shown the past, present and future all at once. How is that? How can I know what a person did a year ago or ten years ago? How can I know what they will be doing a year from now? Their angel knows and reveals it to me through the dimension of time. Since the angels are on God's perfect time, what I call GP Time, they don't always give the exact day or moment of something that may happen.

Because you've all bought into the concept of linear time, you *believe* you're caught up in this illusion. You *believe* you "don't have enough time" to accomplish all that you've planned. You *believe* "time is running out." Therefore, you create that illusion in your life. When you slow down, take a deep breath and *know that your mind controls time,* you can accomplish all that you desire.

The wonderful thing about life in the physical is the experience of linear time and space. You have a delayed response from what you perceive in your mind to what you create in matter. Most people do not see the relationship. They do not realize that *they are responsible for every aspect of their lives.* Time gives your soul a wonderful opportunity to plan, create, review your creations, gain knowledge from them, then plan and create again. Souls in the spirit realm can think a thought and it is instant reality. Only in the dimension of matter can you experience that delayed reaction. Time allows you to cooperate with the Creator in learning how to manipulate energy and manifest matter. You mold God's Energy and use it like Play Dough, creating to your heart's desires. When you observe your handiwork and find it lacking, you struggle to figure out how to change it and make it better. Then you create anew.

Some say "thoughts are things." Edgar Cayce states that the mind is the builder of our reality. Your thoughts and feelings create the momentum of energy that brings back to you a reflection of your beliefs. You can't blame your soul for what happens, because you *are your soul*. You can't blame other people for what happens. You make the choice to *give them your power and allow them to create your reality*. And you can't blame yourself because *you are doing the best you can* with what you know *in this moment in time*. So, who do you blame? No one. It is simply the law of cause and effect in action. What is, is. What you can do is change your view of your physical reality if you don't like it. You *can change your mind* and in some cases, literally transform your life.

Your soul may have agreed to allow another to influence you, (the personality), at some particular time. You may have critical, domineering parents or spouses who seem to take away your ability to make choices. But in giving them that power, you have made a choice. It may be for any number of reasons: you may owe them a debt of servitude or faithfulness. But you must also understand that you can change it if you choose. For example, no one need take physical or emotional abuse from another. Yet, you've all met someone who can't seem to break away from an abusive relationship even when it may bring about their death. As unjust as this may seem, perhaps *they were the abusive one in a previous lifetime* and are now experiencing in full the other side. Yet, by the time a person comes to me, they're ready for change, and knowing their past life helps them *to forgive themselves* and the abusive partner. From this, they can move on and change their lives for the better.

Fate, Luck or Destiny?

There are those who believe in fate. They look at it as the unexpected turn of events that everyone faces in life. Some believe that they are destined to be or to do something special. Others label accidents as fate. People are too quick to give up on themselves because they believe they have no control over their lives – they blame their "bad luck" on "fate."

Yet, consider this: if a clairvoyant can see into the future and know in advance that an event will happen, is it possible to change what is seen? Yes. Yet, it is always the individual's choice. An example of a foretelling of the future is the chronicles of Nostradamus. Hundreds of years ago, he began describing many events through the centuries that would occur, including the rising of Nazi Germany and Hitler. But the world would not tolerate a Hitler for long and would overcome that fate.

Is life preordained? What about free will? These are questions I have asked myself and the way I understand it, both are correct. While in the spirit world, there is no feeling of time and space. All is now. This is why your angel knows the whole story. They can see the past, the present and the future. There are some things that are planned for your life by your soul before you are born. You, your soul and angel set up the life to bring together certain people and experiences to help you learn things from the events experienced. *Yet, we always have the choice as to how we will react to these events.* It's as if the soul has the story outlined, but the personality writes the script.

Time is a relative experience. Again, it depends on your perspective. You've all experienced how time drags when you're anticipating some event to occur. And on the other hand, it's been said that time flies when you're having fun. It's as though your whole being gets caught up in the element of time, projecting your mind into a future expectation or mulling over a grievous past. Either of these will slow down time and make it intense. But when you experience the joy of the moment, you feel like it flows quickly. On that same vein, when you are caught up in a moment of fear, time seems to go into "slow motion" or stops altogether.

A friend of mine related a time-altering experience that reflects fate, luck and destiny all rolled together. While on the expressway, a vehicle several cars in front of her suddenly went out of control. She felt that her angel took over the wheel and steered her car in a zigzag motion to miss the others that had piled up in front of her. In so doing, other cars were able to follow her and avoided what could have been a terrible multiple car accident. She remembers only that "time stood still." She felt as though she moved in slow motion. All of her attention was on that moment. She came through it unhurt. Yet, others died in the "accident." What she experienced was being projected into the "no-time zone" of spirit. She probably did indeed allow her angel to take over.

Edgar Cayce is another example of one who transcended time by lowering his brain waves to the Theta state. It looked like he went to sleep. But when asked questions about a client, he could see that person even if he were hundreds of miles away. He could describe the client's surroundings exactly. Cayce used healing remedies that ranged from ancient herbal medicines to modern-day drugs. Edgar, in his Beta mind, had no knowledge of any of this. Yet, time had no hold on this spirit from the no-time zone. When we realize that our spirit/soul has the same access, we may begin to trust the ideas that flow from it.

There is a season for all things. There is a time to be born and a time to die. There is a definite amount of time given to each person to fulfill the Divine Plan for their life. The soul knows it, even if the human mind does not. Yet, I have heard that some people have delayed the time of their death. One lady says her mother was supposed to have died three times. She had terminal cancer – and beat it. She was in two car accidents that the police said she should not have survived – but she did. Did her soul change its mind? Or was it simply *not her time?*

Time and change are one and the same. It brings the unknown. Change causes stress for many people who like to stay in the comfort zone of what is reality to them. Changing jobs is considered one of the top sources of stress. The commitment of marriage is another "unknown" factor of change that causes stress. Perhaps that's why so many people simply live together. But is it less stress-ful? I doubt it. The anxiety of change lurks beneath the surface if there's no stability to a relationship. The psychological commit-ment of marriage lessens that anxiety for some, but obviously ac-cording to the divorce rate, does not dispel it. Yet, many marriages stay together because the stress of change is thought to be far greater than the stress of a dysfunctional relationship. I know of many older couples who have slept in separate bedrooms for years. They hardly talk to one another and rarely on a heart-to-heart level of intimacy. How sad. Yet, time brings change whether we accept it or not.

Fate, luck and destiny all reflect the fear of change. Fear of financial instability, fear of criticism, fear of love lost, fear of lone-liness, fear of what people will say contribute to a person's inabil-ity to experience the joy of the moment. People get so caught up in their pain that they can't push through it to see clearly. They can't meditate and go within for the fear traps them in the past or the future and robs them of the Now.

The Law of Non-Resistance

Change is a given. You can count on it like breathing. When you fight it, you can make yourself miserable. When you flow with it, the little thorns seem to soften. But change is good even if you choose to fight it. It allows you to gain wisdom from errors and so-called mistakes. To demonstrate this abstract idea, I'm going to weave a little story. It demonstrates how "fate" and "change" and "time" are all tied in together to bring you knowledge that in turn reaps you either wisdom or more doubt and fear. Love and trust brings wisdom and increases your inner peace and joy. Fear brings turmoil, indecision and unrest.

Janet and John: *Scenario Number One*

Janet awoke startled. She swore when she saw she was al-ready late for work. "Damn! The alarm didn't go off!" She flew out of bed and finished dressing on the way out. "No time to fix lunch," she thought. "That will tick John off." Janet sighed heavily, thinking about the fight she and her husband had the night before.

Weaving in and out of traffic, Janet cursed the slow movers as "Sunday Drivers." As she pulled off the expressway toward the city, the right front tire blew. Janet slammed her hand on the steering wheel, her anger rising to a fever pitch. She pulled over to the side of the road, hoping someone would come along and change it for her. "Yeah, fat chance," she grumbled, getting the jack and spare out of the trunk. Glancing around for a place to call her boss and not finding one, Janet shrugged and thought, "He's angry with me already. This will be the third time this month I've been late. Damn!" Janet fumbled with the jack, dropping it once in her haste to get the job done. With sweat beginning to dampen her dark suit, she cursed the tire as it was removed and the spare put on.

"Where the h— have you been, Janet?" The boss exploded in her face the minute she walked through the door. "You're always late. Keep this up and you can stay home! Now get to work on the Harris account. It has to be done today."

"But I'm already working on three other accounts," Janet stammered. The look on her boss' face was enough to chill a cup of coffee. Coffee. Janet grabbed a cup to steady her shaking hands, fumbled with the papers on her desk and spilled the coffee. Tears welled up in her eyes as she wiped up the mess. *Dear God, help me,* she whispered. Janet gulped in a deep breath, closed her eyes and rubbed her temples. The rest of the morning went quickly and uneventfully.

At noon, the rumbling in Janet's stomach reminded her that she hadn't brought lunch. "Who has time, anyway?" she mumbled angrily, deciding to work through to make up for lost time. Just as she began the Harris account, the phone rang. As she listened to her doctor's prognosis, Janet exclaimed, "Oh, no!" Her doctor was surprised that the confirmation of her pregnancy test should cause such a reaction. Janet hung up abruptly, frantically trying to figure out how to tell John. "He'll really be angry," she thought. "If he weren't so tight with the money, I would have bought more birth-control pills. But he'll blame me anyway. He'll say we can't afford another child. John probably won't speak to me for a week." With her head in her hands, Janet let the tears roll silently down her face.

Janet and John: *Scenario Number Two*

When the alarm went off, Janet pushed the snooze alarm, snuggled next to John and dropped back to sleep. She dreamed that she was running to catch up with her daughter who kept disappearing ahead of her. The alarm jerked her back to reality again, and she got up quickly to not awaken John. Dressing hurriedly, she realized that she was going to be late, but took time to pack lunch for herself and her husband. Before she slipped out of the house, she blew a silent kiss to her two-year-old son who was sleeping like an angel. Peace and contentment settled over Janet as she sent up a prayer of thanks and gratitude for all her blessings.

Traffic was extremely slow, making Janet even later, but she drew in a deep breath, turned on the radio and listened to soothing music. As Janet emerged onto the ramp, the right front tire blew. Janet sighed and stated matter-of-factly, "Guess I'm really going to be late today. First, I'll call a serviceman and then I'll call the boss and let him know."

Just as this thought materialized, a car pulled over and a young man emerged. "Can I help?" he asked. Janet was amazed and grateful as the young man finished with the tire and refused to take her offer of money. She still found the nearest phone and let her boss know what had happened and that she was on her way.

As Janet entered the office, her boss, Jim, anxiously followed behind her saying, "The Harris account has to be ready today, Janet." Janet smiled and reassured him that it would be ready. Her quiet voice and unruffled manner seemed to calm him. "I know you've been given extra work, Janet. We do appreciate the way you seem to handle things. You can count on a bonus if you can get that Harris account sealed."

"Are you putting that in writing, Jim?" Janet teased. "Go on. Get out of here so I can get to work." The morning passed quickly until her stomach began to rumble. "Time for lunch," she thought. "I could keep working, but I'm going to take a break. It'll help clear my head." She took her lunch into the conference room where the quiet, order and beauty of the place relaxed her.

"Hey, Janet!" a coworker poked his head in the doorway.

"How'd you and John like tickets to the game tomorrow night? I can't make it. They're yours free if you can."

"Wow! That's great, Mark. Thanks. I'm sure John would love it." Mark's head disappeared and the room was quiet and peaceful once again. Janet was called to her office for a phone call just as her hour ended. It was her doctor confirming the pregnancy that she had suspected. "I'll have to call John. He'll be so excited," she thought and added, remembering her dream, "And I just know it'll be a girl."

The great difference between these two scenarios is in how Janet reacted to time. While the first Janet fought against the events of the day, building up her own agitation and stress, the second Janet did not resist, but took each moment in stride, looking for the beauty around her to help calm and sustain her. Resistance to change compounds the negative and increases stress, leaving one feeling out of control. Nonresistance allows one to flow in the stream of life and come up in charge, on top and ahead of the game.

The Terms of Time

"Time waits for no one" is a belief that you've missed something, or that "time is running out," and you won't be able to accomplish all the things you wish. This feeling of anxiety hits everyone at one time or another. Some people call it the "Mid-life Crisis" while others simply feel like they've "Missed the boat." There are so many clichés that express fear about time. For example, the prudent admonition, "A stitch in time saves nine" refers to a wise use of the moment. If you put off that task you need to do, it becomes a burdensome chore later on.

"Spending Time" People often refer to time as a precious commodity that one "spends" either foolishly or wisely. It's as though they have a huge Time Bank in the sky with a limited account. If they "run out" they feel they're going to pay dearly for it in some way. Do you have to pay interest in purgatory or some place like it? Do you have to work extra hard for the time you "goof off?" Is that why some people feel so guilty when they simply rest and do nothing? Why have we made Time such a task master and we the victims of it? Granted, the physical seems to offer us only 24 hours in a day. Yet, each of you have experienced days in which you seemed to accomplish much more than others. Why is that? Is it because you choose to "take your time," and enjoy the moment? Is this maybe a secret of those successful people who seem to accomplish so much in a lifetime? You bet it is.

"Wasting Time" Where do we come up with these clichés? Is there a waste dump for non-recycled time? When you do something just for the fun of it, or just because you need to do it, is that "wasting time?" When you treat yourself to a movie, or read a good book, or simply sleep an extra hour or two on the weekend, are you to be punished for it some way? Yet, if you believe you're "running out of time," you will feel guilty.

"Time On Your Hands" "I can do that when I retire. I'll have time on my hands then." Time is an illusive Imp that slips away from you until you feel you've missed out on the "good things of life." This little Time Imp tries to manipulate you into believing that it is a "jewel more precious than any other on Earth." Don't be fooled! Time is an illusion. It differs with each person by how it is perceived. There is only the now moment that can be lived through a choice of love or fear. All the following moments will reflect this. When you focus all your attention on the task at hand, it seems to go faster. Because you're not thinking about something else, wishing you were somewhere else, you seem to get through mundane tasks faster.

It's like Mary Poppins singing "A Spoonful of Sugar makes the medicine go down. In every task that must be done, there is an element of fun." It is our approach to the task that makes it "take an eternity" or "Snap! The job's a game." Again, Christ's words come back to guide us: "Unless you become as little children, you cannot enter the Kingdom of Heaven." That inner kingdom is within us. It is that "peace that surpasses understanding." It is a child's eye view of time. Become a little child playing the game of life, pretending, believing in guardian angels, believing in yourself.

"Time And Time Again" "How many times have I told you...!" "Time and time again you. . ." How exasperated we can become with people who don't want to jump when we say jump! The kids never clean up their rooms when told. Your spouse doesn't do the chore you requested. The boss expects you to do his work when you're already overloaded. And on and on it goes.

Yet, part of the value of time is **repetition**. As a teacher of many years, it never disturbed me to repeat a lesson for someone who may have missed it the first time around. Even the curriculum included "review" lessons. Life does that automatically for you. Because you go in cycles as seen in Chapter Four, you are able to view repetitive experiences from a different set of beliefs each time. That is if you're growing spiritually. If you're not, you can get stuck in the same belief and repeat the same thing over and over and over. Rather boring. Wouldn't it be better to continually strive to look at life as a series of football games: same players, same field, but different plays, different reactions, different outcome? It is always your choice.

"Time Immemorial" or **"Time Out of Mind"** refers to a time before recorded human history or human memory. Although not heard very often anymore, when someone says, "This has been in effect since Time Immemorial, they're really saying, "Where have you been, stupid? Didn't you know that?" People often exaggerate. The sarcastic put-down utilizes exaggeration and has been around since "time out of mind." We have to be out of our minds to think put-downs are funny. "Hey, look what the cat dragged in?" or "Cute dress. In fact, real cute." The sarcasm rips your heart with pain. While teaching junior-high students, I made it a rule that put-downs were not allowed in my classroom. It took the kids a little getting used to, but the atmosphere in the room improved daily as they did. They began to realize that no one would criticize them or judge them unkindly. What a difference that made! Become aware of your inner put-downs. Be kind to yourself and others.

"Stands the Test of Time" says when in doubt, wait and see what happens. Don't act. For example, a friend of mine said I just had to go see this psychic who was coming to town. I did. He told me I was a nun in a past life. I already figured that. He told me I lived in the time of the Atlantians and flew "crystal-powered space crafts." I liked that. He said the "Space Brothers will be ready to take up the chosen 144,000 when the Earth changes occur." I frowned quizzically at that one. He went on to say that these cataclysmic Earth changes would wipe out most of the population, but since I had come to see him, I was one of the chosen.

Fear galloped through me at that one. What if he was right? What if the Bible statement that talked about someone in a field being taken up while the other remained was true? What if I were suddenly whisked away and no one knew what happened to me? What if. . .?? I calmed my racing heart and listened within to my angels who said, "Be at peace, Beloved. We are here." The psychic said all this would occur within the year. I waited, going about my business, but in the back burner of my mind, wondered and waited. Two years passed and I figured the "Space Brothers" must have changed their minds. I wondered what this man told those who still followed him. . .if any did.

Songs of Time

Songs have been sung about time as long as man/woman have existed on the planet. One of the more recent ones, (within the past century), is "To Everything There Is A Season," by Pete Seeger, who took the words from the Book of Ecclesiastics:

"To everything (Turn, Turn, Turn) There is a season (Turn, Turn, Turn)
"And a time for every purpose under heaven. A time to be born, a time to die;
"A time to plant, a time to reap;
"A time to kill, a time to heal; a time to laugh, a time to weep. . .a time to build up, a time to break down;"

While we're on the Pendulum of Opposites (see Chapter Three), we'll experience all of the above and more. It's always fascinating to me to listen to the words of songs. I guess being a music teacher may have something to do with it. In this next one by Michel Legrand with Marilyn and Allan Bergman writing the lyrics, you will again hear the cycles of life that relate to the ending of a love relationship. It reflects the pain and questioning all of us have experienced in "The Windmills of Your Mind."

"Round like a circle in a spiral, like a wheel within a wheel, never ending or beginning on an ever spinning reel,

"Like a snowball down a mountain, or a carnival balloon, Like a carousel that's turning running rings around the moon.

"Like a clock whose hands are sweeping past the minutes of the face, And the world is like an apple whirling silently in space,

"Like the circles that you find in the Windmills Of Your Mind!"

We could not complete this song list without including the star-crossed lovers of Romeo and Juliet. Larry Kusik and Eddie Snyder wrote the lyrics to this lovely song by Nino Rota that became the theme from the movie, *Romeo & Juliet*. I have sung "A Time For Us" many times for weddings during my organist/choir-director years.

"A Time For Us someday there'll be when chains are torn by courage born of a love that's free. A time when dreams so long denied can flourish as we unveil the love we now must hide.

"A Time For Us at last to see a life worthwhile for you and me, and with our love through tears and thorns we will endure as we pass surely through every storm.

"A Time For Us someday there'll be a new world, a world of shining hope for you and me."

Perhaps these lovers met in a future lifetime and had the joy of their love shared. They certainly didn't in that time period. Some masters of mysticism say that we come together in a heaven-like world beyond the physical called the Astral Plane. It is there that lost love is found. How nice it would be to know that we really don't miss out.

"The Hands of Time (Brian's Song)" is another sad love song also by Bergman and Legrand that reflects on time as it steals life away.

"If the hands of time were hands that I could hold, I'd keep them warm and in my hands they'd not turn cold.

"Hand in hand we'd choose the moments that should last: the lovely moments that should have no future and no past."

"Now Time" or "God's Perfect Time"

If it is true that you've chosen to be here in this game of time, you can begin to release all the anxieties that relate to it and experience the angelic position of "Now Time." When I'm given information that relates to the future, I'm not always sure when that time will be. I have to tell my clients that spirit doesn't compute time like we do. If it shows me "two" it could mean two weeks, two months or two years. Our souls have an angel who guides them and neither one tells time very well. Since they're on God's Perfect Time, we might as well be, too. That requires a sense of trust in the Divine Plan for our lives. Our view of life is only moment to moment. Our soul's view for our life sees beginning to end. Our angel has access to past lives and more. And God's knowledge of who we are includes even beyond that because we are one with All That Is. When we understand that we are primarily spirit functioning in a physical body, we begin to sort out what is important and what isn't.

There are some things you cannot change. Most often, it's the people in your life. Try as you may, the ones you love will continue on the path of their soul's devising, bound and determined to experience what they will. Yes, you do influence others, but you simply cannot change them if they choose to remain as they are. Putting your ideas of behavior on another is setting yourself up for disappointment. Expectations relating to time are one of the biggest detriments in a relationship. I remember one lady saying she would give her boyfriend one month to make up his mind between her and another. She had one agonizing month and he chose the other! Accepting people as they are is a giant step toward accepting time and the flow of life's cycles. Accepting yourself as well can eliminate a great deal of anxiety and stress. That doesn't mean you shouldn't strive to become all your soul has planned. It means accepting the fact you're doing the very best you can right now.

Time has an illusion of beginnings and endings that haunts us throughout life. It seems that we "can't wait" for something to begin or "can't wait" for something to end. Yet, the flow of life merges all these events into one long chain of experiences that mold and form life. It is how we *perceive the moment* that gains us wisdom. See it in fear and we slip into the murky waters of illusion. See it in love and we are lifted into the joy of the Now.

A simple example of this comes from helping my husband build an addition to our home. Joe had me hold the measuring pole while he used the transit to figure elevations. It's quite a boring job, but it just happens that I was working on this chapter at the time. (I try to pay attention to what has come through from my angels). I stood perfectly still, holding the rod and tuned in to the sounds of nature around me. I heard a blue jay's call and a whippoorwill. I watched a tiny tree frog hop in the ditch where I was standing. I saw the sunlight play tag with the trees. I practiced being in the moment. When Joe said to move here or move there, I refocused on listening intently to what he was saying. All during this I did not allow my mind to shift back to this chapter which I was itching to complete. As a consequence, my usual impatience did not rule my mind and stir up my gut. I felt a tremendous peace and tranquillity surround me.

Living in the Now moment enables you to experience the joy of it without pulling in the pain of past events that may cloud your picture. Releasing doubts and fears about your ability to "get through" the challenge at hand also enables you to live in the Now. The creed for Alcoholics Anonymous is to focus on getting through each minute, then each hour and then each day. They cannot look beyond that or they'll become discouraged and give up. We are all addicts to "Time." To overcome that addiction, our angels encourage us to live in the Now.

The joy of focusing on God's Perfect Time, (GP Time), is that you begin to see the good in each person, event and adventure that walks on your stage in the drama of your life. You actually look forward to the new adventures your soul has planned for you. You know you will be given all the help you need to accomplish what is asked of you from spirit. Loving the Now helps you feel the triumph of conquering your thoughts of doubt and inadequacy. Your mind becomes free to create the kind of life you and your soul really want. And the angels are there as your cheering section, always rooting for you and encouraging you on.

How do you overcome the pain of despair and depression? By living in Now Time. Thoughts run rampant with anxieties and fears that become compulsive. "What will people say?" "What will happen if. . ." "How will I ever. . ." "If only I had. . ." All of these kinds of questions bring on depression. In a way, it is feeling sorry for yourself. Joe calls it "sitting on a pity pot."

The "poor me syndrome" makes one a master of inflicting guilt trips. You may hear words like, "You wouldn't say that if you really cared about me," or "You would do that if you loved me." If you get what you seek, the person does your bidding. But what happens when they don't buy into that guilt trip? What do you do when they say something unkind or they didn't do what you asked? Do you believe that they don't love you? Isn't it like saying, "Poor me. Nobody loves me. Nobody appreciates me. If they did, they would act differently toward me. Poor me. Poor me."

If you're looking for praise, appreciation, love and attention, don't look to others. You will always be disappointed. It's those expectations again. And you're living in a future experience that *you* have dreamed up. Live in the Now moment. Appreciate yourself, love yourself, praise yourself, pay attention to yourself and you will enter your inner kingdom and feel that unconditional love from your angel that will lift you up and bring you joy.

The Secrets to Taming Time

1. Concentrate with full attention on the moment.

There are a few simple secrets to taming that wild element of life called Time. The first is to **concentrate your full attention on the moment**. Anxiety is created when you're impatient with the moment's task because you're looking forward to the next event. "I can't wait 'till. . ." sets you up for anxiety, stress and often disappointment. Somehow things seldom work out exactly as you plan them. Oh, you can become successful in many accomplishments, but most executives will tell you even if the end results are what they planned, the path to it was unpredictable. Once you accept that life is unpredictable, you can flow with the changes that occur.

Being in the moment covers even your eating habits. How often do you sit down to a beautiful meal and eat it without paying a bit of attention? Your mind is on what happened that day. You get angry remembering the offenses of the boss or coworker. Is it any wonder that many people have indigestion or that they are over-weight and underfed? People in the United States eat more than any country in the world. Yet, many are malnourished. We spend mega-bucks on vitamins, believing that it's our food that is lacking. It isn't just the fast food binge. It's also the lack of attention we pay to the food that fuels our bodies. If we took more time to chew each bite and savor the flavors, perhaps our bodies would respond by being healthier and happier – and so would we. Eating is just another example of being in the moment. Jesus reminded us that it's not what we put into our mouths that can hurt us, but what comes out of it. And our words come from our thoughts and fears.

2. Allow your Angel to plan the details of your life.

The second secret to taming Time is to let your angel plan the details that lead to results you desire. You plan what it is you want the outcome to be, then let it go. Don't try to plan every little thing along the path. Don't constantly bring it into your mind to reaffirm it. Since you cannot see the whole picture that your angel can, you do not have all the facts necessary in good decision-making. You cannot get into the shoes of all the people who may be involved in creating your end result. This is where your angel takes over. It can plant the seeds of an idea for a friend to be somewhere at a certain time that will coincide with your needs. That's where the word "serendipity" comes in. It's being in the right place at the right time with the right attitude of joyous anticipation. It is ready for changes, even eager for them. It is ready to step through the door that opens on opportunity. It isn't afraid to ask for help and grasps the hand of the angel that offers it. It sees beyond the physical and into the spiritual, trusting that its soul, its angel and the entire universe are there for support and to bring only good.

3. Let go of expectations of yourself and others.

When you set your hopes on someone else to meet your needs or to react to you in a specific way, you're setting yourself up for disappointment. If you expect your spouse to do some chore or errand for you and he/she forgets, you become angry and disappointed, feeling that you are not important enough for him/her to remember a simple favor. If you are always doing things for others and then when you ask for a favor, they haven't got time, you can feel let down. If you are a people pleaser or a peacemaker, you can become quite upset when someone treats you badly. If you set goals for yourself and others, you could turn them into possible failures that create anger, apathy, discontent and even depression. This is not to say that you should not set goals. But anytime you become too specific, setting deadlines, spelling out exactly what you plan to do – your soul and angel will step in and change things – just to let you know that although you may think you're completely in charge of your life all by yourself, you're not! Putting expectations on yourself or others places you in a precarious position. It sets you up to let you down. Meditate on this and see if you are caught in the expectation trap.

Summary

When I give lectures, people say they feel my joy. They are lifted up by it. They comment on how much energy I have for my age. I was not always this way. I learned it through study and practice. You can do the same. Discipline your mind to live in the joy of the moment. Give 100% of yourself to each minute, each conversation, each task, each chore. Don't allow your thoughts to skip into the future or fall into the past. Stay in the now. I have always believed that people are more important than things. As my children were growing up, whenever they needed my attention, I stopped what I was doing and listened to them with every fiber of my being. I looked into their eyes. I heard between the lines.

It is this focus of attention that I realize now has been part of the reason I am now a psychic. I've trained myself to "tune in" when someone speaks. My musical background also taught me to really listen, to hear all the instruments of the orchestra, one by one. The exercises given earlier are for the same purpose. It is a way of focusing on the moment, of living in the Now.

I had often wondered what Christ meant when he said it is much easier for a poor man to pass through the eye of the needle than for a rich man to do so. I knew he meant that some people can get so caught up in the fear of lack that they make their possessions like chains around their necks. They're afraid of theft so they put locks on the doors. They're afraid they'll never have enough money, so they're always saying, "I can't afford that."

I found out many years later that the parable Jesus spoke of above referred to the gate into the city which was a narrow archway called, "The Eye of the Needle." A rich man had to unpack his camel of almost all his possessions, walk the camel through and then repack it. Makes more sense now, doesn't it? And we're a lot like that. When we burden ourselves with anger, expectation and fearful beliefs and opinions, we're going to have to unload all that extra baggage before we can go into our Inner Sanctum quickly and easily.

The master showed us how the lilies of the field never worry about what to wear each day. They don't worry about impressing people or pleasing people. They live in the moment and rejoice in the goodness of it. So, too, should we. All of our needs will be met. Our life is really right on track. Our train will not leave without us. Honest.

Journal Entries for Week Five

Directions: Listen again to side one of the tapes all this week. You may choose to stop the tape after the relaxation and simply allow your angel to take you where it will. When you have finished your meditation, write down your impressions in your journal. Choose one or two questions each day to meditate upon and write about.

1. List two examples of how you may have "wasted time." Change your viewpoint and record how you may have saved time instead.

2. Study the stories of Janet One and Janet Two. List the references to time in each one. Which one had more concern for time?

3. List some of the things that Janet Two did that made her day more pleasant.
4. List the chores you hate to "spend time" doing. How can your angel help you change your viewpoint and make them more fun?
5. Describe a time when you were late for something and it upset you greatly. How do you view this now?
6. What would you like to do if you "had all the time in the world?" Brainstorm and list as many things as come to mind.
7. Describe how you feel about "spending time" writing answers to all these questions.
8. Make a list of your accomplishments in this life so far. Include the small successes as well as the big ones. List your school achievements in academics, sports, music, etc.
9. Make a list of the events in your life where time dragged or you felt depressed. What would you do now that could change those moments?
10. Make a list of the events in your life when "time flew." How could you increase those joyful moments?

Chapter 6
How Do I Interpret My Dreams?

Guardian Angel hear my call.
When I fall asleep, where do I "fall?"
I sometimes dream I'm flying free.
Are you also flying there with me?

Do we fly together hand in hand
Over trees and sea and land?
How do you know when morning calls?
Do you bring me back – up from my "fall?"

Dreams – The Angels' Game of Charades

Dreams are a wonderful game of Charades that you play with your angel. You recall the symbols in a silly, mixed-up dream and then figure them out. It can be fun. Everyone has a list of words that they use like clichés. Some people say, "I'd give my right arm for that contract." In their dreams, they may see themselves armless and wake up believing they are going to have an accident where they'd lose their arms. Instead, their angel is showing them they are getting the contract they desire. It is also showing them how their speech *can create* what they say – literally. Watch those words!

Dreams are truly gifts from your angel, like a letter to a beloved soul. You need to look at them as your angel coaching you sometimes gently and sometimes rather abruptly. But too often, people see dreams as evil spirits haunting them. They believe they are being chastised. So often, people who come to me with their dreams have translated them into criticisms of themselves. No wonder they become discouraged and give up on their dreams. You must remember that your angel never criticizes or condemns. It is offering you instead little gems of wisdom. If you could only imagine the amount of knowledge you can garner from your dreams, you'd be going to bed earlier!

Dream Research

You may believe that you do not dream. Research has shown that everyone dreams every 90 minutes. Most people don't remember their dreams. In a laboratory situation, people were wired and monitored. When they began a dream, their eyelids would flutter and you could watch their eyes moving from left to right as though they were following the action of a movie. They called these "REM's" meaning Rapid Eye Movement. Shortly after entering REM, the dream scientists would awaken the patient and ask what they had seen. The person gave fantastic accounts of other-world like experiences and claimed how *real* it had seemed.

When you dream, you go to the Alpha Brain Wave level as described in Chapter Two. You go from the conscious level into the lower brain waves into deep sleep and then back up again to an almost wakeful state. Sometimes you wake up, but often you just drift back into the lower brain wave levels and continue to sleep, never even remembering that you had awakened. The Alpha level is that period just before you awaken when dreams come. The trick is to wake up, but stay in that brain wave in order to capture the dream.

Famous Dreamers

Dreams have been helping people for centuries. The Bible records a dream where an angel told Joseph not to be afraid to take Mary, his fiancée, as his wife even though she was pregnant, and Joseph knew he wasn't the father! His belief in angels and dreams was astounding. And he did it a second time when an angel told him to pack up his wife and child and move out of the country! Would you do that? I seriously doubt it. But Joseph did it a third time when the angel gave him the "all clear" sign so that he could take his family home again. All in dreams. Amazing!

Daniel of the Old Testament gained quite a reputation as a dream interpreter and was later saved from a fiery furnace by an angel. Inscribed on a stone tablet before the Great Sphinx of Gizeh in Egypt around 1450 BC is a dream that Prince Thutmes felt was important enough to share with his followers centuries later.

Dreams and dreamers are sprinkled through all ancient cultures and writings. Greek mythology placed great emphasis upon dreams. Aesclepius, the god of healing, was called upon to grant a dream that would tell the person how to heal the body. There is a 3,800 year-old papyrus scroll in the British Museum that describes specific details of how to interpret dreams.

Thomas Edison is said to have taken many "catnaps" especially when he was working on an invention. He claimed that he often awoke from a nap with the solution to his problem.

If dreams have helped mankind so much, why do most people never bother to study them? It's like receiving letters from your dearest friend that you never open. Your guardian angel is your best friend, and it wishes to communicate with you through your dreams.

Dreams – An Angel's Tool

Do you ever wonder where you go when you sleep? I do. I've read that people "astral travel." This means that after they go into a deep sleep, their physical bodies are put on auto pilot and left behind while they *consciously* fly to any place they can imagine. How I've wished I could do that. Maybe someday. If we do go somewhere while we sleep, do we visit with our angels? I'd like to think so. I have come to believe that my dreams are scraps of conversations with my angel. In spirit, we don't have to use words but instead communicate with thought transference. When my spirit body comes back into the physical body, I have to translate that journey and conversation into word symbols so I understand it.

Dreams are a useful tool for angels. Even though dreams seem scrambled and confusing, decoding them reveals precious gems of wisdom. In 1978, I began an intensive seven-year study of my dreams, recording them in detail. After ploughing through dozens of books on dreams, I found only a couple that met my criteria. I didn't feel that anyone could tell me what my symbols meant. When I looked up something in their dream dictionary, it gave Freudian meanings or something else that seemed unreal to me.

My study of dreams taught me how to interpret them by looking at the symbols, people and events as a play on words. For example, if you dream of Rosie O'Donnel, it probably doesn't mean you will meet her, but rather, you need to lighten up and look at the funny side of life. On the other hand, if you dream of Cher, you may be gently reminded to share what you have with others.

Most often, dreams give us a new look at our lives, helping us see from another perspective. For example, when I dreamed of driving a large truck, worrying about how I could handle such a big load, I took it to mean that my work was overwhelming me. I needed to slow down and look at it from a different perspective. I realized that I was trying to do all the work in putting on a music program that dealt with rehearsing over 150 students, making props and costumes, writing the program, etc. When the principal asked how she could help, I was delighted to "share the load." I felt like I was right on track again and the program was even better than I had hoped. My angel was sending the message that my load was too heavy, and it sent the help as well!

Ways to Remember Dreams

I've learned several techniques for remembering dreams. When you make up your mind that you really want to remember your dreams – you will. As you begin to fall asleep, ask your guardian angel to help you recall one that you will remember and understand. You should prepare yourself by having a notebook with pencil and flashlight, if necessary, by your bed. No matter what time you awaken, lie perfectly still and almost drift back to sleep. When you recall a dream, describe it in your mind as you review it. Then move carefully as you get your pencil and paper and write it down. Use the present tense as though you are still in the dream and it is happening now. Write as much detail as you can remember.

Later, when you reread the dream, you will notice the words themselves give you clues to what your angel is telling you. This is why dream dictionaries are not as helpful as you may believe. Your angel uses your vocabulary and clichés to paint the dream. Remember to interpret your dreams in relationship to your daily events. Add them as part of your journal and you will begin to see how they relate, answering questions you may have asked in regard to something of importance.

Another method is to have a tape recorder handy by your bed. When you awaken with the dream, move slowly as you speak into the recorder. Keep your eyes closed as visual awareness can snap you back into the Beta level and erase the dream. In the beginning, dreams are very fragile and can dissipate easily. You may believe you will surely remember because something seems so vivid and real, but they will vanish in the rush of everyday events. Later, as you practice remembering your dreams, you will easily remember them and will have as many as five or six each morning. I did. It became almost too much for my mind to grasp and too much time to write them out and then interpret them. I actually had to beg my angels to slow down and help me interpret them without writing them down. They did.

Ways of Interpreting Dreams

There are two ways that work best for interpreting dreams. One is to tell them to a friend. By listening to your own play on words, your friend can bounce ideas back to you. Together, you can begin to see what message your angel has for you. But if you try a dream dictionary, make sure the interpretation feels comfortable. You will feel an "Ah ha!" within when you make a hit.

The second way to interpret a dream is through what I call scripting. Some dream therapists have people act out their dreams setting up two chairs. The person asks a symbol in the dream why it is there. Then he gets up and goes to the second chair and immediately responds as that symbol, saying whatever comes to mind. I decided to do that on paper by writing out my script. You do this by first going to the Alpha level of mind and then write your dream in as much detail as you can. Next, write in script form your questions to whomever or whatever in your dream. It is important to keep it in your journal so you can see how it relates to your everyday life. Once you let go of your own preconceived ideas about the dream, you can allow your angel to speak to you indirectly with amazing wisdom.

Five Kinds of Dreams

1. Dreams of the Future – Precognitive Dreams

Dreams can foretell a future event. They're called *precognitive dreams*. I had one that I certainly didn't interpret as I would like. I dreamed of three numbers in a box. I knew it pertained to the lottery, but since I had never bought a ticket before, I called my friend who knew all about it. Karen patiently explained to me how to "box" the numbers, where to go and how much to bet. All the time she was telling me this, I had the feeling that it was not me who was supposed to do this, but her. I knew she bet on the illegal "street" numbers, but didn't have enough nerve to ask her to do that for me. So I placidly went ahead and followed her directions. Nothing happened. I called her and asked what to do next. She said to continue for the next three days. I did – and nothing happened. Meanwhile, Karen bet those numbers on the street and won a couple hundred bucks. Needless to say, I was a little miffed, but figured it was my own darn fault for not speaking up.

Then later, I realized that the numbers were really for her and not me. I had been following my angel's guidance well and didn't even know it. It seems that the part I play in Karen's life is to pop in at unexpected times – just as she needs me. Once I arrived expecting her to give me a reading, (she is an excellent psychic), but found her rushing to the hospital where her husband had gone earlier with a heart attack. I took her and stayed with her. After this kind of thing happened several more times, I got the hint from my angel that I was to be reading for her, not the other way around. In my innocence and lack of knowledge, I looked up to Karen for her esoteric background. As time went on, I realized that I may not have as much knowledge, but my soul was filled with great wisdom that I was just beginning to discover.

Another precognitive dream came before I was to give a lecture to 300 people. I dreamt that the overhead projector wouldn't work. Next, I found myself in the bathroom, looking in the mirror. I had a white substance all over my face. When I awoke, I realized that the dream could be warning me about something. I interpreted the white substance as symbolic of having "egg on your face."

When I arrived at the auditorium, I asked that the projector be checked out, but everyone was too busy to do it. When I offered to do it myself, I was put off. Sure enough, when it was time for my lecture, the darn thing wouldn't work. But in remembering my dream, I remained calm and joked with the audience while the maintenance people scrambled to repair the machine. Because of my dream, I was able to pull it off *without* egg on my face.

2. Dreams That Reveal Our Fears and Emotions

Probably the most important thing that I have gained from my dreams is an awareness of my fears. My angels had been trying to get through to me about them for years. Then they made a breakthrough when a nightmare jarred me awake in the early morning hours. My heart was racing so fast that I didn't want to get up and record what I had witnessed. But with pencil and pad, I reluctantly crept out of bed and began writing. I had no idea how profound this dream would be in my life. I recorded it as follows:

I am in an attic room battling a huge rat the size of a tomcat. I have a stick and am trying to keep it from biting me, but it keeps lunging at me. Suddenly, I jam the stick into the ugly creature's eye and it writhes in pain. I dart around it and rush headlong down the stairs. Below is a public building with all kinds of people around. I scream, "Get out! Get out!" Everyone scrambles through the large glass doors outside to safety, but I can't seem to leave.

I wrote out in script form a conversation with the rat in my journal. After writing the dream in the present tense, I spontaneously wrote as shown below without thinking about it in advance:

Betty Rae: *Rat, why are you in my dream? You are ugly and you frighten me.*

Rat: *Your fears are frightening you. I represent all you fear.*

Betty Rae: *But why are you attacking me?*

Rat: *Fear attacks the very fiber of your being, debilitating you and hindering your spiritual growth. You hold me off with your sticks, but you haven't really confronted me. Even trying to kill me doesn't get rid of me, nor does running away.*

Betty Rae:	*I don't understand. How can I get rid of you?*
Rat:	*Confront me. Recognize me.*
Betty Rae:	*How do I do that?*
Rat:	*Remember how you put the stick through my eye and twisted it into my brain, believing surely that would kill me?*
Betty Rae:	*Ugh! Don't remind me!*
Rat:	*The eye represents the way that you look at things; the brain represents your interpretation or perception of things in your conscious mind. It is the way your conscious mind "sees" which causes you fear and creates your monster. Recognize that and you will be free of me.*
Betty Rae:	*Why was I in the attic first and in a public building below?*
Rat:	*The attic represents your mind or thoughts, while the public building represents your encouragement for others to "get out" their dreams. You will make this knowledge available to them in the future.*
Betty Rae:	*That's amazing, Rat. Thank you!*

Needless to say, I was astounded by the insight and wisdom that came from this so-called "nightmare." It has been shared with so many people since then in helping them to understand themselves, their dreams and their angels. The dream was not only a tremendous help to me, but was also prophetic.

3. Dreams on a Physical Level

A dream that was so obviously symbolic of my physical state of being was demonstrated in the following:

I am in the passenger seat of a station-wagon filled with my students. One child reaches over the front seat and plops a wild boar on my lap. I'm appalled. It's so ugly! But I reach down on the floor and pick up an apple and place it in its mouth. The children are singing happy songs.

When I awoke with this little gem, I grabbed my notebook and wrote it down, chuckling as I did so. One could interpret this dream to mean I was going to a pig roast with an apple in its mouth and all. Another could say I was "learning" about how to roast a pig since there were "students" in my dream. What came to me was none of the above.

Betty Rae: Pig, why are you in my dream? You're a bore that's ugly and not even cute like a real pig.

Pig: You've said it, not me. You're being a bore with your old eating habits, making a pig of yourself, stuffing your face with fast foods and fattening junk. Uck! You certainly aren't cute, that's for sure.

Betty Rae: I suppose you know that I've been thinking about being a vegetarian lately. Is that another reason why I found you so ugly? The thought of eating something as ugly as you is quite repulsive!

Pig: Yup. You've got it! Giving yourself, (as a "pig"), an apple was a good idea. Fruits and vegetables with beans and nuts would make your body sing.

Betty Rae: Thanks, friend. I'll give it some serious thought.

It was obvious in this dream that a play on words was the key. I was not "in the driver's seat" which would mean being in control of my life. My eating habits were definitely out of control. I had been ignoring my own inner self for quite some time. There were "students" behind me, symbolic of a lesson "behind" this scene.

4. Dreams on the Spiritual Level

All dreams are for our spiritual growth, but sometimes we're given a dream that is clearly spiritual. When I awoke from the following dream, I was in awe of what came to me in my scripting.

I am rescuing a large lamb buried under snow beside a curb in front of my home. I take it by the scruff of his neck and lead him to my backyard, fearing all the while that he might bite me. But as we enter the fenced area, he changes into a bird and flies away.

My scripting went something like this:

Betty Rae: Lamb, who are you and why are you in my dream?

Lamb: I represent the Christ within you. When you befriend others, even those who may harm you, you befriend me. When you lead and teach others, you give them freedom. Don't be sad when they fly

*away. You have given them wings with your kind-
ness and guidance. Rejoice and be glad.*
Amazement and joy filled me. This had been the farthest thing
from my mind.

In another dream that became a spiritual gift, a road taught
me how to relax. Yes, I said a road. I dreamt about a lovely, serene
country road. That was it. Nothing else. I asked the road why it
was in my dream. It told me I needed balance in my life: rest,
exercise and fun. I had been trying so hard to interpret my dreams,
I had overdosed on them!

5. Dreams of Past Lives

I dreamt once of being in a box seat to the left of a stage
where three women were singing. The first one was a stout, dark-
haired woman, the second an African-American woman and the
third an American Indian. Suddenly, the first woman took off her
head and exchanged it with the second who took off her head and
gave it to the third. It astounded me so that it took awhile before I
understood that these women represented past lives. I majored in
voice in college and was told I should pursue a career in singing,
but I opted for marriage, a family and teaching. This dream presented the possibility that perhaps I had been an opera singer in
another lifetime and, therefore, desired to do something different
this time around. Another simple symbol that is represented in this
dream is the fact that they were to the left of the stage and so was I.
In my many spiritual consultations or readings, which are very
much like dreams, if I see something going to my left, it means the
past, while going to my right means the future. Yet some research-
ers have said just the opposite. This is why *you do the interpretation* according to your own brain's data bank.

Some dreams of past lives can seem so real you may believe
they are something that is going to happen in the future. When a
lady came to me for a reading, the angels showed me a past life
drama where she had been abducted by a neighboring Nomad tribe.
I described the scenes in detail as they were presented to me. It
was as if a video camera had clicked on in my head.

I saw her as a young girl dancing before her father, a king, in an elaborately decorated tent of red velvet and gold. When the dance finished the king gave her in marriage to the older man who sat beside him. The girl didn't appreciate this reward for her talent, and in outrage, fled from the tent, mounted her stallion and raced into the night.

She was abducted by a warring tribe and taken to their camp. They were angry with the king for having conquered their land. When they realized they had his only daughter, they thought they could barter and trade. But as the king's army poured into the camp, killing everyone in sight, they realized the king would rather destroy his own daughter then give into them. They stabbed her in the stomach and fled.

Just as I related this part of the story to the woman, she cried out as though I had stabbed her. Then she told of a recurring dream where she was being stabbed in the stomach! She said it had haunted her for years. She believed this was something that was *going to happen to her.* Her fear debilitated her, keeping her from doing many things like simply going for a walk. She called to thank me weeks later, saying that she had been miraculously freed of the dream and chronic fear.

I have given you examples of my method of interpreting dreams through scripting. It requires your being in a meditative state by following the directions in Chapter Two. Immediately after writing out the dream in the *present tense*, begin scripting it. You do this by writing a question to anyone or any*thing* in the dream. You could even ask a chair why it's in your dream. The secret is to use your playful imagination to allow the chair to respond *without thinking about it ahead of time.* Clear your mind of your interpretation of the dream and allow yourself to respond spontaneously. Many a time I thought I knew just what the dream meant until I scripted it out. I am always amazed at the insights that come to me. I am convinced it is my angel and my soul that speak to me through my dreams. They can for you as well.

Day-Dreams
I used to get scolded for "Day-dreaming your life away!" But

I had so many "What if's. . .?" that I found such fun to think about. For example, back in the early forties, I wondered "What if someone could build a rocket ship that would take people to the moon?" Little did I know that someone else was day-dreaming about that very thing. As I hovered near the radio to hear *The Shadow*, (before television was invented – I told you I was *old*!), I could *see* "The Phantom" in his purple cape appearing out of nowhere to rescue some poor damsel in distress. I would sit for hours playing with my small glass collection of dogs and cats and pretend that they were families. I built houses out of dominoes and cardboard shoe boxes.

I still remember listening to a spooky radio show where ghosts were tapping on the hull of a ship. My mother turned it off because it was "bedtime." All my frustrated arguments wouldn't convince her to turn it back on. I think *she* was scared. I still wonder what happened. It gave me many "What if's. . ." to think about.

Day-dreams can scare us, too. When I worried my family would disown me if they knew I was a practicing psychic, I was day-dreaming all kinds of scenarios. When I was "found out," they were upset at first, but they've come to accept me as a little eccentric and love me anyway. None of my "day-dreams" materialized.

Once I learned the difference between "good" day-dreams and "bad" ones, I became more discerning. Good ones are fun because they play with ideas for solving problems – seeing how many different ways you can do it. Many of my good day-dreams have become reality like my first hooked rug, (but I'll save that for the next chapter). "Bad" ones are surrounded by fear and plunge you into icy waters that hide your angel.

In order to even begin to day-dream, you have to awaken the right side of the brain. It allows you to visualize various paths to take in making a decision. It helps you to "see" what the outcome would be if you go a certain way. Joe uses day-dreams to perfection. As a supervisor on jobs where he had to estimate time and materials, he would sit high up "in the steel" and go through the "What if's. . ." in his mind, visualizing different ways to save the company money. His success at this gave him a reputation that became a legend as "Little Joe." Each morning Joe, now retired, but still very busy building our home, has his quiet time when I've overheard him saying to himself, "If I take..." and sometimes his hands move in the air as his mind goes through the visualization. In sharing this segment with Joe, he said, "It's called 'Thinking Ahead' and you can figure out what the consequences will be."

Ah, what if more people had that ability....

When my eight-year-old grandson came for a visit, I was reminded of my own three sons at eight, seven and six. Jack had no concept of the consequences of his actions. When he shoved his sister off the riding lawnmower because it was "My turn!" He didn't even look back to see if she was all right. When he stuck the "Pick-Up-Sticks" upright in the carpet and was ready to "bomb" them with a hard ball, I had to explain to him what might happen. When he turned the faucet on the island sink around to spill over on the floor, I had to explain about consequences. The image of "Denise the Menace" and "Home Alone" kept popping in my mind and reminding me of my own sons years ago when I had to ban the "Three Stooges" from our home. I had caught them bopping each other on the head and attempting to poke eyes out! One son today at almost forty can't get enough of "The Three Stooges." It's his son who visited! So much for day-dreams.

Visions

A vision is an image that comes without previous thought about it while a day-dream is a wish in picture form that comes from a thought. The difference between the two is that the wish is vague and ever-changing, while the vision is sometimes startlingly real and can take an unexpected turn of events. Once you understand how to meditate and go within to your Inner Sanctum, you will receive visions from your angel that will enlighten and encourage you.

I didn't always know that difference. When you have developed an imagination like mine that easily conjures up images of anything my mind can grasp, you think it's *all* imagination. It wasn't until later in life that I began to see the difference. Now when images "pop" into my mind, I know it is a gift from spirit and not just my imagination. When I awake from sleep sometimes at three or four in the morning with an image in my mind, so clear I can touch it, I know it isn't my imagination. When I receive new ideas about something I know nothing about, I know it is a vision from spirit. In the next chapter, I give many examples of this.

Visions can be like waking dreams. You don't know where they're going and are surprised at the unexpected twists and turns they can make. For example, in a meditation, I saw myself walking along the seashore when suddenly a dolphin rose from the depths and playfully danced on the surface. He was beckoning me to join him. Without hesitation, I plunged in with the impression I could breathe in the beautiful waters of clear emerald green. I was thrilled to touch the silky smoothness of the dolphin's skin. But I had the impression it wanted to take me somewhere. I grabbed his back fin and we silently slipped though the water. I marveled at the beauty of the colorful fish and shell life as we zipped by.

Soon we were rising to the surface in what looked like a cave opening into bright sunshine. On the shore was a being of bright light with its hand out for me to grasp. It led me to a lush green clearing where there was a circle of light beings, even brighter than my guide. I was ushered into the center of the group and became aware that it was all the great master teachers. My mind wanted to verbalize and record this awesome event, but I was silenced and told simply, "Be still and listen." I felt tremendous love and energy that radiated from this group. It seemed to levitate me.

Without warning, the entire group disappeared and my guide led me to a large, pillared white building where I was ushered into what felt like the Presence of God. I sensed a throne of brilliant gold surrounded by beings of even greater light than before. I felt such wonder and reverence that I fell to my knees and put my head to the floor. I don't remember anything more until my guide touched my shoulder and I found myself back on the seashore by the cave. My dolphin was waiting to take me home. Just recalling that vision fills me with great peace and joy. I'm not at all clear what it means, but somehow it doesn't matter. I felt too humble to even ask.

Dreams + Meditation = Visions

A dear friend of mine came to me regarding her dream of being shot by a man with a paper bag over his head. This dream was reoccurring and frightened her. With the help of another technique, we unraveled this mystery. I helped her relax and took her into meditation. Then I directed her to "walk into her dream without fear and confront this man." She did so while I held her hand. As she approached the man, she noticed that he was wearing shoes like her own. When she tore off his mask, she discovered "he" was indeed herself. We asked the man why he was in her dream and was told that my friend was "shooting herself down" by her own words and actions. She recalled how she often used the term, "That just kills me," or "I'd die for that." She also revealed how she had been praying for spiritual growth. Her angel used the "death" scene to show a dying to old ideas and a rebirth to new. She indeed was going to experience spiritual growth. That understanding of a play on words was a giant leap for her spiritually. She began to see her life in different terms and became more careful with her words.

This episode of interpreting a dream from a meditative state and *extending the dream to a conclusion* was new to me. I thanked my angels for guiding me to help others in a new way. I found it fascinating. We could actually enter into our dreams and gain more knowledge. Dreams became a source of wonderful meditations in the future. One in particular I will add here even though it is quite lengthy. I include it because I encourage you to use this technique. I have gained so much knowledge from it that it is worth sharing.

I awoke from a dream with a joyous feeling of love. The dream was about a walk with a being of light. This incredible dream-meditation was given to me about twenty years ago while I was parked in a campground by myself with my computer. I was trying to decide what to do about my marriage. My pain and grief had consumed me and I needed to get away. I had gained such solace from journaling with my computer that I packed up the whole thing, (and back then computers were quite large and cumbersome). I was gone for five days. It was on the last night that this dream came. I immediately went to my journal and wrote out what I had seen and felt. The dream went like this:

Walking through a thick forest, I observed patches of golden yellow blend with dark green, like invisible spotlights on a stage. My feet crunched loudly in the quiet stillness. Up ahead, a large shaft of light seemed to beam a stairway to heaven. Drawing closer, I perceived a translucent figure dressed in glowing white smiling at me. I hesitated, a little frightened, but when it stretched out its hand to me, I grasped it. The sense of joy I felt erased all questions of fear or doubt. "Where are we going, Sir? And what should I call you?"

The being of light wore a long white robe. He was tall with dark flowing hair and a strong chin. He seemed to be glowing as if he were lit up from within. I wondered if it could possibly be the Christ, but could not allow myself to believe it.

"I am your guide and friend, dear one. Be patient. You will see," the light being answered, his voice gentle.

I couldn't let it go. Was it Jesus? Did I dare ask? "Are you my Guardian Angel?" I asked impatiently, avoiding the real question.

"In a way. I have been with you since the beginning." His smile sent warmth flowing through me. "Choose to make patience a strong point," my guide urged.

Startled, I answered, "Oh, ah. . .okay. I'll try." What else could I say?

My gentle friend sighed, looking so sad that I felt alarmed. "You carry such a heavy load," he said, staring straight ahead.

I looked around, wondering who he was talking about. "What load, sir? I haven't brought a thing with me, not even my purse."

"Allow me to help you become light enough to travel with me," he gently urged.

"Of course," I responded eagerly, alarmed at not having the foggiest idea what he meant. Light enough? Darn it, I scolded myself, why didn't I stick to that diet? Are we going to fly somewhere maybe? I wondered. Then I worried about those things I had to take care of tomorrow. And I really should let the family know if I'll be gone long. They might worry. . .

"Will you release your future and follow me?" His step slowed

and he looked directly at me.

My eyes dropped from his gaze. I hesitated, thinking about my plans for the future. I had wanted to finish my Master's Degree. I wanted to learn to paint with oils. I wanted. . .I looked at my guide, wondering, Where are we going? I noticed the wood lilies nodding their heads, encouraging me to say, Yes! I smelled their delicious perfume, remembering the story that Jesus told of how this perfect flower had all its needs met. I knew he would take care of mine as well. Yet, making decisions was difficult. What if I made a mistake? Everyday I am confronted with choices, from what to eat and what to wear to whether to speak or remain silent.

"Is your way good for me?" I asked. "Is it God's way? Are you of God?" I grew fearful thinking maybe this person could be the devil in disguise. Then I felt a little embarrassed, yet knew everyone should be cautious. That was wise, wasn't it?

"Yes, little one. I am a messenger from God."

A thrill went through me. Still, I hesitated, my forehead a mass of wrinkles, trying to figure this thing out. If this was my Guardian Angel, I wanted to follow his advice everyday, not just now. "How do I tell your way from my own, sir, in each daily decision?" I recalled how many times I thought I had made the right choice only to discover that I had blundered again.

"If you decide to follow me, you'll always hear my voice, but through intuition or inner urging, not always in words like this." This beautiful spirit grew brighter and love filled my being as he smiled patiently.

I had read about learning to listen to your "gut" or "hunches." Was that like my guide's voice now? "But how do I know it's you?" I asked, thinking that it was just too easy to fool myself.

"Test anything by asking what God would have you do. Then wait until you have a strong feeling of joy within you about the direction that you should take. Sometimes you perceive what I suggest as impossible because you want to map it out the way you think it should go. Release your way, allowing God's perfect plan to unfold. You'll always be happily surprised."

"Okay," I decided. "I gladly release my future into your hands.

I will follow you." My body suddenly jerked and I staggered. I felt
like I had been carrying a heavy backpack that was pulled from my
shoulders. Was this what he meant by being lighter? I wondered.
But there is no backpack!

I realized that we were standing at a Y in the road. I chuckled
thinking that even roads ask "Why?" Which road would we choose?
I questioned again. The one on the left looked good, with its wood
lilies and daffodils. I couldn't see too far down the road on the
right because it curved and vanished from view. My guide took my
hand again and led me to the path on the right. Again I chuckled,
shaking my head. It figures, I thought, wrong again.

While walking beside this wondrous being, my impatience and
curiosity mounted about what would happen next. We rounded another bend, and I stopped abruptly in front of a small, luminous
spaceship resting in an open field. I shivered with excitement as I
felt this pulsating craft that seemed to be alive with its radiating
glow of light.

My new friend turned to me and without any warning asked,
"Will you go on a mission that will take you around the world?"

My heart almost popped out of my mouth and I squealed,
"Yes!" without thought or hesitation. I was ecstatic with joy as I
flew over to the little ship and stood on tiptoe, trying to see through
the glowing glass. "Oh, yes, yes!" I blurted out in one breath. "Of
course I'll go." I was trying to figure out how it opened so I could
get inside when the light being spoke again.

"You are still too heavily laden, dear one."

My heart dropped like a hundred ton rock down into my toes.
Heavy? My mind staggered. Heavy? I guess so, if he won't let me
go after all. I hung my head as my friend gently led me away from
the glowing craft to a grassy spot where he urged me to rest. I
plopped down, dejected, ready to burst into tears. "Please, sir, just
tell me what to do and I'll do it."

This great and gentle being sat beside me and put his arm
around my shoulders as he began to explain, "Your past experiences burden you with unresolved embarrassments, angers and
misconceptions. Release them."

Flashes of my childhood, of my alcoholic parents, of my adoptive parents, of being torn between two families, of Todd's cruel words all jumbled together. "How do I release the past?" I was confused and almost in despair. "The past is past. How do I release it? And to where? How do I reprogram all those repeating tapes inside my head?"

"Command that those flashes of memories that tug at your mind, 'Be gone!' Will that they be released into the Divine Light. Picture them being dropped into a large glowing dumpster where they can be changed into good. Change your view of them from this moment. Then forbid your mind to dwell on any past error or pain any longer."

"You mean. . .make up my mind to. . ." I heard the simplicity of it and felt its power. I remembered Edgar Cayce saying that the mind is the builder. I recalled James Allen reminding us that we are what we think and thoughts are things. All these concepts that I had stored on the shelves of my mind came tumbling down to face me. We do create our own world, I thought. Suddenly it all made sense!

A brilliant cardinal fluttered down to a low branch to blink his black eyes at me and tell me that all creatures in nature are in tune with Divine Will. Only humans have the choice to go against it, to create disharmony, to choose fear and chaos in their lives. Why on Earth would anyone choose to do that? I wondered. Because it is Earth, not Heaven, I heard the answer within my mind.

I closed my eyes and firmly stated out loud, "I release all of my errors, my feelings of guilt, any misunderstandings, anger, hatred. . .and anything else in my past that keeps me from the freedom of seeing Divine Light in myself and others." I promised myself anytime I started brooding about some hurt or embarrassment, I would declare, "I release my past into the Light of God."

A flash of memory brought my friend's angry words before me. I felt my gut wrench and my heart hurt. She really had no call to say that, I quipped. She gets mad so easily. She should do something about that temper of hers. I felt my own anger surge up from inside, making my head throb.

*"Will you release the judging of others into the Divine Light?"
Eyes gently probed mine as a hand touched my shoulder.
"Judging?" I cringed. Now I know he reads my mind! My
eyes dropped quickly, embarrassed. I pulled at the long grass, remembering the words of the Christ telling us not to judge lest we
be judged as well. "But, it's such a habit, sir, criticizing and blam-
ing others. You want me to stop, just like that?" My fingers snapped
the air. "How?"*

*"Declare it. Will it so. I will remind you when you forget until
you will no longer be able to judge another unkindly."*

*Quickly, I closed my eyes, vowing, "I do release all judging
into God's pure Light." I turned to my dear guide and admitted,
"And, uh, thanks, 'cause, uh, I'll need help with this judging business."*

*My friend was so patient, but I was beginning to think I would
never become worthy to travel with him. I moaned, I have so many
faults. If we wait until I've overcome them all, I'll never get inside
that spaceship.*

*"Will you give up all fear and negative thoughts into the Di-
vine Light, also?" The gentle eyes pleaded with mine.*

"Fear? Negatives?" Now I was confused.

*The light being gently replayed my previous thoughts, like
rewinding a videotape. I even saw my own body sagging in despair. I was amazed: first, as to how he had done it, and secondly,
at how I had been so negative. "But negative thoughts seem to
creep up on me. How do I even recognize them? And how do I
know what causes the anger I may be feeling?"*

*"Anger, dear one, is most often caused by unfulfilled expecta-
tions," he advised. "Release all your needs and expectations of
another and your fears will leave as well."*

*I was beginning to sound dense as I asked, "How do I do
that?" My poor slow mind felt numb.*

"Will it gone. Declare it released."

*Still not really understanding, but beginning to trust, I de-
clared, "I do will it." I took a deep breath, sat up straight and
affirmed, "I reject fear in all its many disguises. I release all nega-*

tive thoughts and feelings into God's Light."

It seemed impossible that just saying it could really change it. It was just too simple. I was always worrying about something that was going to happen, or not going to happen, like never getting to ride in a spaceship. Uh, oh. I was doing it again. I glanced up at my guide and felt the love and warmth from his smile. He had not judged me. He loved me! Joyously I said, "I release all worry and doubt into the Light." My friend laughed out loud, sending up sprinkles of light like fireworks on the fourth of July.

Gently, my guide pulled me to my feet. With the joy of his presence beside me, we walked toward the glowing craft while he spoke of the great need for people of Earth to help bring divine Light upon the planet. As I listened, I thought, How I wish Mary could be here with me. She would love this. And boy, does she need to release negatives. Every time she opens her mouth. . .Uh, oh. I caught myself and peeked at my friend. Quickly I blurted out loud, "I release judging into the Light!" I was remembering!

The light being laughed again, sending euphoric shivers of delight through me. I was beginning to understand. My guide was helping me catch those errors. I will be able to let go of them, I thought. Does that mean. . .maybe it's possible to become. . .I caught my breath at the audacity of my thoughts. . .perfect?!

"Yes!" my friend declared in a booming voice that startled me. "As Jesus, our brother taught, 'Even as your heavenly Father is perfect.'"

"You mean when I release all this. . .junk. . .and blend my will with God's, then. . .?"

"Yes, little one. Yes!"

I felt like turning cartwheels, running and dancing – and I did! My joy was so full that I ran up and hugged my dear friend. I drew back quickly, amazed at myself.

The burst of joyous laughter reassured me. He reached out and drew me into a big bear hug. "Dear one, it is all right. I am your Elder Brother, and you are so greatly loved. Be not fearful of expressing your own spontaneous love and joy."

It was all right. Everything was all right! Oh what joy! "What's next, Big Brother?" I was bouncing up and down. "I'm ready to release everything. You name it, I'll release it. I feel like I'm really getting into the swing of this."

"Will you release all those you love? Will you let go of your human relationships?" my Elder Brother challenged, quietly serious again.

That stopped me like an avalanche of snow. Does that mean I'm supposed to give up my family just like Abraham was willing to sacrifice his son, Isaac? Does this mean I'm leaving them and never coming back? I can't live without my children, my. . .I caught my thought, stopping myself. Whoa! Wait, I wondered. Isn't that making them gods? "Thou shalt have no other gods before me," not even those you love. Isn't my guide really asking me to make God more important than anyone or anything? I expectantly searched my friend's luminous face and felt him laughing once more. Yep, I'm getting the idea.

But I sensed that he also meant for me to give up my fear of losing love, of losing Todd in our fragile relationship and my fear of losing the love of my children if I did.

"I do release into the Divine Light my family and all human relationships, even my husband, Todd. And I know, dear friend, you'll help me to bear the pain of this relationship and see him and my children as perfect and beautiful beings of light.

"Is there anything more? Am I 'light' enough to travel yet?" I desired so strongly to be in the glowing ship. I was extremely curious how it worked.

"Almost, dear one," Elder Brother answered patiently. "Your heaviest burden I have left until last."

My eyes widened. Was there anything left? I felt I had given up my very soul. I held my breath, baffled as to this biggie that would come crashing down on me.

"Will you release to the Light all your human desires, your Ego and pride, your opinion of yourself?" My brother's shimmering light became like a mirror reflecting my fears of ridicule, my desire for success and my need for praise and encouragement.

"How can I give that up? What are you asking of me? Imme-

diately the answer reached me. "Yes, I do completely empty myself of 'Me.' I release all those things that prevent me from filling up with God's Light."

The response from my Elder Brother came so quietly that I leaned closer to hear. "Including your disbelief that even now says, 'This is just make-believe; this can't really be done? This really isn't happening. It's only a dream.' Will you release all of your doubts into the Light?"

With head bowed, I blinked away the smarting tears, knowing that nothing, but nothing, could be left hidden from this gentle, patient friend. I realized then that I didn't have to know how all of this would be done. By declaring it so, God would do it for me.

Instantly, my feet left the ground as a weightlessness overcame me. A joyous electric tingle flowed through my body, causing me to float upward, right into the radiant ship. I saw that I was dressed in a glowing white garment, kind of like a space suit of pure energy. I felt safe and secure and euphoric.

I looked down at a golden belt that surrounded my waist. My eyes flew to the dials, buttons and computer to my right. There was a globe of the planet that seemed to be alive as it pulsated and breathed.

"What do I do now?" I eagerly asked. "How do I start the engine?"

Elder Brother smiled a beam of radiance that caught my breath. "Visualize yourself radiating God's Light outward." He pointed to my golden belt. "Focus from this Light center at your solar plexus. Send it out to anyone or anything in need of love and healing. Picture them as perfect. Picture any situation as perfectly resolved."

"I can do that?" I asked incredulously. The nod from my light-being friend confirmed it. I felt a power surge within the craft. "Yes, I know I can." A tv screen to my left flashed pictures of places around the globe – war, famine and destruction. As I touched the screen, it opened into the scene! I jerked my hand back and the scene faded.

The whole idea overwhelmed me and doubt blurted the words,

"Can I really do this? And how will I know if I'm making any differ–?" I regretted the words before I'd finished the question. I felt my body sag, felt the power whoosh out of me and my craft. But I raised myself up, took a deep breath and firmly declared, "I release all doubt into the Light."

Hearing that joyous chuckle, I turned shyly toward my dear friend as he affirmed, "You'll be given confirmations as you need them. Don't look for results. Trust and believe."

Reflecting from my TV screen, I watched my body reacting like a sensor balloon deflating and folding in upon itself when I was filled with negatives or doubts, and then filling up and becoming buoyant and light from encouragement and positive thoughts. "That's me?" I asked incredulously, pointing to my reflection.

"That's you, my dear Betty Rae. Be at peace and know you will always be guided."

"Aren't you coming with me?" I asked anxiously.

"No. There is room only for you in your spaceship."

My eyes caught my body deflating and I breathed deeply as I watched it fill up again. Amazing!

"Now, let's see," I looked at the controls of my little ship. "To activate my spaceship, I simply think of someone who needs God's Light and Love?" It sounds a little too simple. I thought. What are all of these gadgets for?

"Not only think of them, but picture them. Make an act of your will to create good within them, healing them with Light, opening their minds and hearts and souls to God's plan for their lives."

"You mean kind of like activating their own spaceships? If all the people of the world were open to God's Light within them. . ." I tingled as the thought sent joy galloping through me.

"Use all the instruments within your ship to look into any part of the world you choose. Use your imagination and your ship to correct a problem or heal any wound. Whatever you need will be provided."

I can't wait to tell all this to my friend, Mary, I thought. I can just see her mouth hanging open. . .My face and ears began to burn as I looked to see my friend's head cocked to one side, keenly observing me. I sighed, knowing I had "oopsed" again.

"Be cautious, dear one," my Brother warned. "Remember to direct all your intentions for the glory of God, for the good of all concerned. Avoid trying to add to your own glory. There are many who are not ready for these truths. They will reject them and you. Wait and listen for my guidance."

I felt my shoulders beginning to droop with embarrassment. "I do so want to share this adventure with someone. Does that mean I'm only trying to 'blow my own horn?'"

"No, dear one. Your desire to be of service has not gone unnoticed. Many will be sent to you to hear what you have learned, and at the most unexpected time. As you recognize my voice, you will easily discern what to do or say in all situations."

With a contented sigh, I settled back, closed my eyes, feeling confident and comfortable inside my little "Bubble of Light." I wondered where to send God's Light and Love first.

I suddenly felt the spaceship lift, unsteadily at first, but then it began to soar. . ."Anyone or anything. . ." The words echoed and reechoed and repeated themselves in my mind. Instantly, I found myself in a strange land. . .

The park's lawnmower roared through my mind, canceling out everything. I snapped my eyes shut again. *Please don't go, dear Brother.* I pleaded. *Please let me stay.* But it was all gone. I had abruptly returned to the here and now. But I had recorded it all on my little computer just as it had occurred. I knew I could enter my spaceship anytime I chose. I knew I would do it again. (This dream and meditation were triggered by "The Effective Prayer" given in Chapter Two.)

Summary

Every waking or sleeping moment is a gift from God. When we joyously approach each day with excited anticipation of new discoveries, we know we're connected with our soul and angel. Some of you may shake your head and decide that you can't learn all that has been given in this guidebook. You may believe that you don't have enough time, or you're not smart enough, or you've got more important things to do. Whatever. It is always your choice. You can give up now and never find out all the treasures of wisdom and joy that your angel and soul have buried deep within you. If someone offered you a brand new Mercedes would you say, "Oh, no thanks, I don't have time to drive it and I sure wouldn't take it out in this traffic." If your angel offered you a million-dollar strand of pearls, would you say, "Oh, no thanks, I just don't have time to wear it. I never get dressed up anymore." It is *always your choice!*

Journal Entries for Week Six

Directions: Listen to side two of the tapes again all this week. You may wish to use only the relaxation part and allow your angel to take you where it will. Try to go to the Alpha level without the tape.

1. In this exercise, we will make up a dream and have you script it to give you practice in interpreting it. After you read the "dream" below, close your eyes and visualize yourself within the scene. Feel it. Smell it. *Be it.*

    I am walking along a lovely country road lined with huge oak and maple trees. It is summer and the sun is warm and the road is dusty. I watch my bare feet scuffing slowly along. I feel at ease. I'm in no hurry. Suddenly from my left a deer leaps across my path, startling me. It scurries to the other side and turns to look at me. As my pounding heart stills I am mesmerized by its lovely black eyes.

    Begin by asking any object like the road, the trees or the deer a question. Without thinking ahead, write out an answer as quickly as you can. Ask any more questions you desire for clarification. Ask another object why it is in the dream. Thank each one for the insights they have given. Thank your guardian angel for helping you with this exercise. Remember to ask for a dream tonight.

2. When you remember a dream, follow the directions for writing it down and then script it out like a conversation. Write without allowing the left side of the brain to analyze any of it.

3. Create an extension of the dream through a state of meditation. Relax deeply and then bring to mind your dream in as

much detail as you can. Walk into that dream and change it for your greatest good and better understanding.

4. Do this exercise also with an incident in the past that caused you pain. Treat it like a dream, taking it into meditation. . .*and changing it for the good of all concerned.* Write in your journal what you have seen and heard.

5. Create your own Dream Dictionary. As you begin to understand the symbols used in your dreams, write them down. Note how many times they're used.

6. Write out a list of Day-Dreams by beginning a statement with, "What if. . ." Take one or two into meditation and allow your angel to give you insights about it.

7. Become aware of those "Visions" that pop into your head from "Out of the blue." Write about them in your journal.

8. Anytime you have trouble visualizing or meditating, review this book and play one of the tapes. Believe in yourself and your angel.

Chapter 7
You Say I Created This Mess? No Way!

Dear Angel of my inspirations,
Fill me up with beauty and love.
Join with me in all my creations,
That I may reflect God's Peace and Love.

In all the tasks I do this day
Turn the old into something new.
Inspire in me a brand new way,
To create goodness through God and you.

Shakti Gawain writes, "Creative visualization is magic in the truest and highest meaning of the word. It involves understanding and aligning yourself with the natural principles that govern the workings of the universe and learning to use these principles in the most conscious and creative way."

Creativity: The Child of Solutions

Angels have inspired us with ideas through many forms, but most often when we are searching for a solution to a problem. Most people think of the word "creative" as belonging to artists and writers, etc. I understand creativity to mean looking at a situation from a different viewpoint. Most people come up with two ways to go: either/or. With your own Angel of Creativity, you can come up with a third alternative or even a fourth that no one usually thinks about to encourage freedom of choice. This reduces the stress of feeling trapped in a situation with no way out. There's always an alternative. And there's always a solution to every problem. My life is a testimonial to that.

When I was laid off from teaching, I figured it would be a snap to find a job. Todd was always tense about money and in the previous year, I had talked him into purchasing a new house. We had depended upon our two incomes to make the payments. Well, I couldn't find a job. With a Master's Degree, everyone said I was "overqualified and under-experienced" – even to sell furniture! Although Todd was beginning to panic, I wasn't. After a long period of trying sales jobs, I turned to secretarial work and loved it. But it paid only by the hour.

Finally, I found a salaried position helping laid-off auto workers find jobs. I became a "job developer." Rather ironic, don't you think? It was my sales experience that landed the position. My skills as a teacher of music were worthless. But my *training* as a teacher, which included organizational skills, promoted me from job developer to office manager. They wanted me to completely revise their procedural manual. I was given the task of preparing the company for an audit. Although I had no real secretarial skills, they put me in charge of the office staff. They taught me how to use a computer. I was called "Brain-Storm Betty," because I always came up with unique ideas to solve simple or complex problems. I had learned to get out of my angel's way to allow ideas to flow.

Mindsets: Blocks to Creativity

Mindsets are beliefs that get stuck in the brain, and even when we know they no longer serve us, we hold on to them for comfort like a baby's pacifier. Mindsets shut out our angel's creative help. When a belief is so strong that it doesn't budge, it blocks a solution otherwise not thought of. We simply have to *let go* of our way and be open for another. It means going within and asking for help. It means awakening our own psychic abilities to perceive a situation from a higher perspective.

I have met some people who say they are eager to learn how to be their own psychic, but when presented with a new way of looking at their lives, they balk and refuse to budge. For example, one lady came to me wanting to "do something about her daughter." She believed her daughter, Lisa, was stubborn and unreasonable and needed someone to "talk some sense into her." Her daughter was determined to move out and find a job in another city. She had graduated from high school and was ready to conquer the world. I asked her mother what Lisa would use for money to make this move. Linda said, "My husband and I, of course." I pointed out that perhaps if they refused to give Lisa any money, she would figure out what to do herself. Linda wouldn't even hear of it. Apparently they had always bailed Lisa out whenever she had gotten into trouble. The mindset was there. No matter how gentle and patient her angel was, it couldn't get through to her. I didn't even try.

Another incident regarding mindsets is quite vivid in my mind. A group of my friends always went camping together each summer with my little pop-up trailer. Candy and the others would have long debates over which site was the best, usually taking an hour to decide. Candy directed the show, making sure it was big enough, private enough and quiet enough. Once settled, she always staked out her territory on the bunk that gave the most room.

One year, I decided to solve the problem. I found a campsite and set up the trailer before anyone arrived. I also took over the favorite bunk. Something inside me rose mischievously and drove me to do it. I felt light-headed with inner giggles. Once everyone arrived, the silence from the group was heavy with anticipation. All eyes were trying not to watch Candy with her stiff jaw and complaints about the dog barking. Everyone knew that Candy was very angry with me, but she wouldn't say a word.

It took one day before the fur began to fly. That night I drove the four of us, at Candy's request, to our "old site" for a "quiet meditation." Afterward, Candy said she had been "shown" I had to overcome mindsets. I almost burst out laughing, but kept it inside. Candy had set herself up to be our "guru," handing out insights about our faults and how we could overcome them. My other friend told me later that Candy had been commenting to her in the back seat about how nice our "old spot" was, and pretended to hit me over the head with her notebook. I, of course, was unaware of all this. But was I? That night back in our bunks, I again felt driven to speak up. I suggested perhaps her meditation about mindsets was not for me but for herself. I gave examples of her behavior in this regard, trying to be gentle and kind. I really didn't want to hurt her, but once I started, there was no stopping. I told her the group had discussed this before and agreed with me. That night was the breakup of our prayer group. They were disappointed that Candy had such a mindset and would not accept any of the group's suggestions. We mirrored what she so easily handed out.

Every person who comes into our lives brings a reflection of ourselves. If a person has a trait I can't stand, my angels have suggested I look within to find it in myself. Candy helped me see that I often got into ruts with my way of thinking. My many fears were pointed out to me. I really thank her for helping me become aware of my need for acceptance and appreciation. By speaking up, I had to overcome my fears, for I jeopardized those needs. And, indeed, I lost her friendship. But I gained a great deal of confidence in listening to my own needs and my own inner wisdom.

I also have to thank Todd for the gift of mirroring my fear of making mistakes. It seemed when I was with him, my anxiety about his anger brought out more stupid errors and mistakes than anyone else could create. If I was driving the car and Todd told me to turn left, my mind frizzled as I worried about bringing his wrath upon me, so in my confusion I turned right. . .and brought his wrath upon me. When I finally learned it was all right to make mistakes, when I gave up trying to win his love and approval, when I honored myself and my own needs, I no longer needed that mirror. My buttons could no longer be pushed. I was free.

Look at those people in your life who cause you anger. Bless and thank them for being a mirror to you. They are a gift to help you know yourself. They are a great stepping-stone to spiritual growth. But don't believe everything you hear. No one knows you as well as your angel. When another criticizes or belittles you, check to see that perhaps you are a mirror for them to see themselves more clearly. *Projection is a common form of venting one's frustrations.* It's always easier to blame someone else rather than accept responsibility for our errors or shortcomings.

Playfulness = Creativity

While teaching music, I became very acquainted with the

angelic attribute of creativity. It helped me think up the many unusual and fun-filled programs that delighted audiences and students alike. For example, one program involved kindergarten through third grade. Each class wrote an original song about a circus and then acted it out on stage, singing in costume before parents and friends. Another program involved eighth graders who wrote and produced a full-fledged musical with lyrics, original music, costumes and props.

I felt my angel's presence helping me write and publish a set of educational filmstrips with original recordings called *Let's Make Music*. A friend from my college days suddenly appeared in my life and got the ball rolling for the project, even finding a publisher. Then she disappeared again while I wrote the script, sketched the frames, composed the music for the recordings and completed the assignment. It was my first experience with publishing anything. The thrill of having your creativity appreciated in this manner is unequaled.

This angel urged me on when I puzzled over how to make English grammar interesting. Both my students and I were bored silly. As I set out to solve this troublesome dilemma, several new methods of learning through games were created. One exciting job-search simulation was later published with other fun-filled, hands-on writing projects.

Thinking up creative ideas is only the first step. Other teachers thought I was crazy for all the work involved in these projects. After all, I had textbooks and workbooks that gave all the lesson plans I needed. Why did I make so much work for myself? they asked. Because the text books **were boring**, that's why. And I loved doing different things to awaken my students to the joy of learning. Taking one day at a time, I didn't even notice the extra hours or help I gave my students. Neither did the kids. One very bright, but lazy student exclaimed he'd never worked harder in English or had so much fun! That was reward enough. The Job Search Simulation was so successful, parents asked for their children to be put into my class. One parent thanked me for her new job because she had learned how to write a resume from her child's lessons.

Angels Have Agendas

When Joe and I retired, we created a whole new life in the country. I thought my angel of creativity would probably retire as well. I had no idea how wrong I was. After deciding to remodel our home, a misty vision began growing of a special rug for my office where I would do my readings. I began sketching a design of various symbols depicting the spiritual aspects of life such as the Yin/Yang symbol for balance and a rainbow for hope.

The next problem was how to make this rug. I didn't like the shaggy look of latch-hook, so the angel showed me a way of looping strips of wool cloth instead of yarn. I went to the craft store fully expecting to pick up the materials I needed. But no one had ever heard of what I described. I could see it quite clearly in my mind's eye and said it looked like Berber carpeting with cloth loops pulled through a backing. All they knew was yarn and latch-hook.

After traveling hundreds of miles and phoning what seemed hundreds of craft stores, I finally went to the library and found what I had envisioned. I wondered why I hadn't started there to begin with. I discovered that this form of rug hooking went back to the early Egyptians. That began a new career as a "hooker." (Joe has had fun with that!)

After a year and a half, my four by six-foot "Symbols" rug was born and soon afterward was featured in the book, *A Celebration of Hand Hooked Rugs*. It was selected as one of thirty out of hundreds of rugs submitted. I was thrilled. Later I was told that mine was the only rug to have a unanimous vote of the judges. They were amazed that it was a *first rug* and curious about how it had come in a "vision." (I may call it "mine," but I know it was a gift from the angels).

A full-page article accompanying the picture of the rug explained the unusual way I came to create this project. For some of my family, it was their first awareness of my work as a visionary and psychic. It forced me "out of the closet!" As I look back, I can see that **my angel had an agenda** beyond my simple knowledge. This was the beginning of the work I was yet to do. Visions increased and creativity mushroomed.

My angel of creativity showed itself to me as I awoke early one morning. She presented herself as a hooked angel in a flowing, blue-green dress with soft white wings and a rainbow halo. I admired it, but dismissed it because I was working on the last of five hand-hooked projects as part of a teacher-training program. I was determined to complete the five-year course in one year. The last rug was troublesome; I couldn't seem to get it right. But the vision persisted and appeared three more consecutive mornings until I pleaded with her to "wait until I'm done with that blasted Oriental!"

She did not appear on the fifth morning. I was afraid I had offended her and perhaps she would not come again. I felt guilty, but went back to the Oriental, which suddenly began to flow easily. After the last stitch had been put on the binding, this delightful angel awoke me the next morning around five a.m. I felt its urgency and sense of "Do it now!" So I made my rainbow angel (see back cover). After it was completed as a stand-up angel, I "just happened" to notice a call for "Use of unusual materials" in the rug-hooking magazine. By hurrying, I made the deadline. Like the Symbols rug, it, too, was submitted in the last minute. The Rainbow Angel was chosen to be published as well. Now I know why my angel was in such a hurry.

And they weren't done with me yet. About a year or so ago, I felt an inner urge to "Sit down and draw!" It was almost a command that propelled me to gather blank paper, pencil and large eraser. When I sat, I drew a blank. "What would you have me do?" I asked. The image of my daughter drifted into my mind and soon I was sketching a hazy vision of her guardian angel. The eraser was essential because I couldn't quite get the eye-hand coordination to connect with the vision in my mind. I had never even attempted to draw people before. Before I knew it, a lovely angel was playing a lyre on the page. Her large wings flared out behind her. I grabbed some colored pencils and finished the vision. Almost immediately, I thought of my daughter-in-law and another angel pushed its way into my mind and my hands flew as she became visible on the page. What a joy!

This began a short career as an "angel artist" where I sketched my client's guardian angel. It always had something in its hands to give a message unique to the individual. Listening to those angels can be challenging. I did not feel talented enough to be doing what they had asked of me, but I continued to sketch and draw what was given whenever I was asked to do so.

I remember doing a portrait of a little six-year-old boy. His angel looked to be about twelve and would not stand still long enough for me to sketch him. I saw a large table beside him filled with books and told the boy's mother that her son would go on to higher education. I saw that he had quite a task ahead of him that would benefit mankind in some way.

The next shove from the angels came when they urged me to my computer late one night. Within a few days, forty letters flowed through my fingers. The only changes made were my typos. A few days after that, their silent command was to find four by five blank index cards and draw angels for each of the forty letters. I nearly fainted. Yet, I read the letter on trust and a wash of rose-colored love flowed over my being. A vague picture of an angel of blue with pink and green wings and golden halo began to emerge. She held the hand of a little girl angel who was taking her first step off a cloud, ready to "try her wings." Thus began another adventure in following those inner urges, the prompting of angels. Following is the Angel of Trust with her letter.

Beloved Soul,

Rejoice and be glad in all things for they are perfectly reflecting that which you have chosen to experience in this life of the physical. Your Spirit sees past, present and future, but chooses to experience only the moment. It does not judge these experiences as "good" or "bad" but only as knowledge that begets wisdom. It is the purpose of your Spirit to gain Divine Wisdom. Trust in that and be at peace.

Be at peace and know you are Divinely guided upon your spiritual quest. Your path is well-lit although you seem to be in darkness. I am always with you, holding your hand, enfolding you with love, protecting you from harm. Trust in me.

When an idea buzzes in your ear to create something new, dare to trust that it is Divine Guidance, and that you can accomplish it. Release all fear and self-doubt for they are the stillborn infants of creative ideas. Trust that I am with you, sustaining and encouraging you. All is well, Beloved. I walk beside you.   *—Your Guardian Angel*

Angels Create Beauty

Both Joe and I are constantly amazed at how my angels work. If all of this sounds out-of-the-ordinary to you, perhaps it is. But I have learned each of us are encouraged by our angels to create beauty. When we begin to open to their gentle prompting, we can work miracles. I've been paying attention to these divine beings for most of my life. . .even when I wasn't aware of them. They're used to tapping on my heart and whispering new ideas in my mind. They persist even when I refuse to pay attention, like my Rainbow Angel. But angels have agendas beyond our simple visions. This Rainbow Angel became my trademark as a spiritual psychic. It whispered to a "hooker" in Detroit, who was moved to call me for the pattern after it was published in the magazine. When I refused to make a copy of my angel, her disappointment made me blurt out, "But I'll sketch your own angel, if you like." She became a kindred spirit in her love of beauty and God.

Follow That Hunch!

We never know why we suddenly have an urge to call someone. When I found out my younger brother had cancer, I was so upset – not so much about his illness as with myself for not listening to my angel who had prompted me to call him weeks earlier. I knew his angel would take care of him, but because I was "in tune" with him on a psychic level, I felt I had let him down by not being there for him. Even now that cancer has taken him and another brother from my visible eyes, I feel their presence with me, telling me it's all right. They're both much happier where they are now.

Yet, as I look back on my life, I wonder how many other things I could have accomplished if I had let go of my fear of ridicule and failure. I wonder how many suggestions from my angel I have ignored completely. Then my angel's love pours over me and reminds me to release guilt into the Divine Light. I do and joy floods back into my life once again.

Trust

It seems that the other key word for this chapter, besides creativity, is trust. When your angel whispers in your ear, when an idea pops in your head, when you find yourself on the wrong road, when it comes to mind to call your friend. . .follow it; do it; listen to it. It you don't act, your angel's hands are tied and after awhile perhaps it won't try as hard to get through. Angels must wait for us to awaken from our deep sleep of fear, and remember that we are really spirit wrapped in flesh.

Angels create serendipity in life, of being in the right place at the right time when we let go of fear. For example, one lady told me how, on the spur of the moment, she went to see James Redfield at his book signing of *The Celestine Prophecy*. While waiting in a long line that wrapped around a corner or two, she struck up a conversation with the people around her. To her amazement, she discovered an old classmate from high school. Chills ran through them both as they remembered one of the insights stated "There are no coincidences." That wasn't all. Next to her on the other side was a person she knew from her old neighborhood as a child. And it didn't end there. A lady further down the line stepped forward and said that she couldn't help but overhear them talking. *She was also a long forgotten acquaintance of my friend.* When they related this to James Redfield, he admonished them to pay attention and to find time for all of them to get together and talk. There was more to their "chance" meeting.

After I had begun my "Job Simulation," a teacher friend of Todd's happened to come to visit. We discussed his recently published foreign language crossword puzzles. I told him about my project. He suggested I send it to his publisher. I did. They accepted it and asked me for ten more like it to be put into a teacher's book.

If I hadn't trusted that a new idea would be given to me on how to teach boring grammar, the "Job Simulation" would never have been born. If I had doubted that I would be given the knowledge each day on how to follow through what I had started, nothing would have happened. If I hadn't trusted the creative idea of hooking my own rug precisely as I saw it, the failure to find a store could have defeated me. If I hadn't trusted the prompting to take the chance of being rejected and submit the Symbols rug and the Rainbow Angel, they would never have been published – and I would never have touched the lady from Detroit and many others. It goes on and on and on.

Trust means listening to your gut, your intuition and hunches. It means putting aside doubt and even ridicule to follow your heart in what you know to be the right thing for you – not for everyone, but for you. It took a tremendous amount of trust for me to leave a 32-year marriage, the security of a beautiful home, the chance that my family would reject me – but I did. Todd could not accept my spiritual perceptions and resented the time my creative ideas took away from him. He was too fearful of it. He tried to change me. He nagged, scolded, criticized and ridiculed me right out of the marriage. It took trust that my heart would heal, that my family would still love me, that I would be all right.

It took trust to open my heart to another once more, for my angels had an agenda of love for me as well. Some may call my meeting Joe a lucky break. I call it the Divine Plan for my life. It took big-time trust to marry a man I'd only known for six months. But as I look back, I recall the tremendous ESP we had together that first six months. We were always reading each other's mind. We still do it seven years later. But the clincher of this "lucky break" was that Joe was given my name by that student I had in 1956. She had been a dropout who adopted me as her other "mom." Fran popped in and out of my life for 37 years when she brought Joe to me. Coincidence? I hardly think so. Angel agenda? Yep.

It certainly took trust to enlarge upon the creativity of hooking a rug I'd never seen before or drawing angels I'd never drawn before. And recently they have inspired me to create a board game that's called. . .what else? *Come, Play with the Angels*. It's easy to see why I stress **playing**. Worry, anxiety and the other disguises of fear are all the death of creativity.

As a teacher of all ages of people, I've observed that the biggest block to our angel of creativity is our belief system. Somehow we have that famous "mindset" about what we can and cannot accomplish in this life. Oh, I know there are some things outside our scope of talents. I'll likely never go to the moon this lifetime or become a famous scientist. That's obvious. I'm not talking about that kind of thing. I'm talking about becoming the very best of who we are now. It means stretching our minds and hearts beyond our self-imposed prisons of fear. It means being open to learning new things – like a computer, or a language, or a new craft, or becoming a psychic!

Joe's older sister refused to come from California to Michigan for a visit. She said she was, "Too old; too crippled; too afraid of flying. . ." etc. Joe had just turned 70. His sister was 76. For every excuse Valerie made, Joe came up with a solution. "You can take a nonstop flight, Val. We'll have a wheelchair for you. We'll pay for your ticket." He refused to let her make excuses. She came and had a wonderful time, exclaiming over and over how glad she was that she had let Joe talk her into it.

Within Joe's home-remodeling plans, he wants to have a room large enough for all the people that come for my classes and weekend seminars. He's building a wood shop underneath. He's erecting a pole-barn next to the garage so he doesn't have to go out in the snow to get on the tractor that will plow the snow. Joe has never believed he *couldn't do* something. He has always found a way. Like the 1,500 gallon cement septic tank that had to be moved. Joe and his friend did it in one day with a backhoe. I shake my head and marvel at this man. The stories he tells about leaving Malta at the age of 13 and coming to the United States to live with a father who was a stranger; of running away from that home at 14 and being on his own ever since; of having jobs where he ended up in management almost every time, even when he didn't know much about the job; of becoming a legend in his work as an industrial pipe-fitter because he was small in stature, but mighty in mind. But that's another book.

Joe calls his guardian angel his "dumb mind," (meaning "silent" not stupid). It seems that he has always been in contact with his soul and angel. Whenever he has a "problem," he visualizes several ways he could go with it and then lets his "dumb mind" play with it awhile. "Out of the blue" the solution comes to him and he acts. He never acts until he's gone through this process if it's something important. Others might say they "Let go and let God." Same thing. The point is, Joe has used this technique all his life and credits it for his many successes.

Four Elements of Creating

There are four elements necessary for creating our lives the way we'd like. Unless all four are in place, we will not achieve our goals.

First, your **soul** must want to experience a new adventure.

Second, your soul must communicate this desire to your **mind**.

Third, your **emotions** must believe it's possible and become **excited** about this idea that swirls around your mind and heart, teasing you, giving you only glimpses of what could be.

Fourth, as the ideas become possibilities, **you must act**. Your **body** must get up and do what is necessary for anything to become reality in the physical.

So many people complain to me that they have done everything they know how to change their lives, but the same old problems seem to haunt them over and over. They keep finding relationships that are abusive, or they can't find the perfect job, or they never have enough money. . .on and on. When I begin to ask questions, one of the main obstacles I find is they *can't make up their minds what they want.*

My dear friend, Mary, kept saying that she simply wanted to know "God's Will" for her life. "If only God would tell me what I'm supposed to do with my life, I'd gladly follow it." What she didn't understand is that God is always prompting her with ideas and suggestions through her angel, but she thinks they are her own desires. They seemed too "earthy and not spiritual," she complained when she desired to open a home for senior adults. She followed that desire and had a successful business. But she got out of it in only a couple of years, convinced she had failed because she hadn't been financially "successful" or helped people like she believed she should. She concluded that it must not have been "God's Will." When the angels began to point out how she helped her friend, Judy, who was discovered to have multiple personalities, she saw God's handiwork. When they pointed out how she helped an old man feel loved and wanted, she again said perhaps God was working though her. The angels found so many things that showed her how she had really listened and followed her heart. But when she was finished, she was finished and God motivated her to move on. We cannot judge success by the world's eyes. We have to look within to the spiritual levels that only our angel and God know about.

Your heart's desires are what motivate you to try new things, to dare to venture beyond your comfort zone. This comes from your soul and God. They plant the seeds within your being that cause a restlessness until you figure out what is bothering you. Perhaps you are bored with your job and need to find another. Perhaps you need to take a class to stimulate your mind and increase your knowledge. Perhaps you are ready to meet someone new who will challenge you to new heights of spiritual growth. Listen to your mind, body and heart.

Without all of these elements, ideas will fizzle and will be washed out of your mind and heart. For example, if your soul has a great desire to become a millionaire but your belief system is clogged with ideas of poverty, do what you may, it just won't happen. I know of a man who earned close to a million only to lose it – three times. He wondered why he couldn't seem to hold on to money. He would make sound investments and build up a great deal of money. Then something would happen and *poof!* It was all gone. We concluded he had some basic beliefs that were blocking his prosperity. When he investigated further, he became aware he believed money was evil. He had a great fear of bad things happening to him. He also realized he believed he wasn't worthy of great abundance or prosperity. When he was given Catherine Ponder's book, *The Dynamic Laws of Prosperity* (Prentice Hall, 1962), he unraveled those debilitating beliefs and was able to keep the next million he earned. He had all but one of the four elements to create. He lacked the belief he could keep it.

On the other hand, a friend of mine, along with millions of others, has a great desire to win the lottery. She has the belief that she's quite worthy of it and has explained to God how she can help people with it. She goes out each day and buys a ticket. That's three of the elements, but she's missing one more: her soul has no desire to be a millionaire. It did that two lifetimes ago. It wants a simple life of service to others. My friend is always doing things for people and is quite comfortable with the income from her teaching job. But she has a tendency to give money away and always seems to run short when she needs it.

Summary

If you have a great desire to accomplish something, pay attention to your inner thoughts. Listen to your soul. If you have no desires and are perfectly happy just staying where you are, watch your outer world – does it stay the same? If not, pay attention. Your soul is speaking to you through your angel.

After attending "West Side Story" at the Detroit Opera House, I read of a "dream come true" from the General Director, David DiChiera. He spoke of the renovation of the 1922 building with the "newly constructed 75,000 square foot stage, state-of-the-art orchestra pit (large enough to accommodate nearly 100 musicians), and rich acoustical and visual properties." This magnificent building began as an idea of several souls who inspired their personalities to work toward a common goal, raising millions of dollars to bring the joy of music to others.

We are all creators every moment of our existence. As long as we can think, we are creating. We are creating even when we aren't aware. The secret is to begin to know yourself, to listen to your words, to listen to your thoughts. If they're negative, you're creating those uncomfortable situations that come back to you as a result of those thoughts. Listen to your reasons for wanting or doing something. Listen to your angel's suggestions and advice. Listen by going to your Inner Sanctum. Take time to do this and you will know only peace and joy.

Listen to side three of the tapes. Find a quiet place where you will be undisturbed for thirty minutes. For some of you, this may seem an impossibility. It may mean getting up earlier when everyone else is still sleeping. It may mean locking yourself in the bathroom while you take a leisurely bath with your tape recorder! Remember, you made an agreement with your angel. Don't give up now. I know how easy it is to snuggle back into your comfort zone and forget about all this spiritual growth stuff. Remember: *you're worth it!*

Journal Entries for Week Seven

Directions: Practice each day going to the Alpha level and into your Inner Sanctum without the tapes. Use them if you need to. Select one or two of the questions below to use for meditation. Record your impressions in your journal.

1. List some of the projects you have created that delighted you and others. Remember they can be unique solutions to problems or any kind of creative thinking.

2. List any art or writing projects that you remember. What were people's reaction to them? How do you feel about them?

3. How would you rate your writing skills on a scale of 1 to 10? How did you decide this?

4. Have you ever written poetry? How do you feel about it? Make it a point this week to write at least two simple or complex poems in your journal.

5. When you have a disagreement with a spouse or friend and communication breaks down, how do you resolve it? Do you give into them? Do you get angry? Do you speak louder? Do you get quiet? What is another way you could express your needs? What is a possible creative solution that would benefit everyone?

6. Name someone who drains your energy when you're with them. Why do you think this is happening? What do you dislike about this person? What do you like about them? What constructive, creative solution can you and your guardian angel bring to mind?

7. Name someone who energizes you when you're with them. Why do you feel good in their presence? What qualities do they have that you like?

8. Describe an incident when you were prompted to call someone and didn't, but wished you had.

9. List something new you would like to learn. What adventure would you really like to have happen? How about an air-balloon ride, skydiving or learning a new craft? List some creative experiences you would like to learn or accomplish.

10. Take a class just for the fun of it, or study something new.

Chapter 8
What Happens When I Die?

Dear Angel beside me, Light and guide me
As I leave the physical world this night.
My life's light is dimming, Divine Breath is thinning
My soul calls me home.

Beloved Child, I stand beside you, to light and guide you
as you leave the physical world this night.
Your life's light is glowing, Divine Breath is showing
Welcome, Beloved! You are home!

This last chapter investigates beyond physical experiences into the realm of spirit. It explores often-asked questions and reveals many facets of Divine Truth. Obviously, you are aware of the world of spirit beyond the physical or you wouldn't be aware of angels. Angels are changing the way people think from a materialistic, science-only viewpoint, to an awareness of something larger, beyond our limited beliefs. It's what I call "The New Millennium."

Some Christians are steeped in the fear of "an end of the world." The angels give us a more hopeful picture. They tell us there will be changes on the planet – there already have been. When you think of the planet as a living organism that fights for survival like the rest of us, you can imagine "boils" that erupt as volcanoes and earthquakes. It's like a shaggy dog that shakes the water off its back, causing everyone around to get drenched as well. The many so-called "natural disasters" are Mother Nature fighting to save her precious child – Earth.

People are beginning to awaken to their responsibility to our environmental home. The majority of souls on the planet have been in their intermediate stage of understanding how the physical world works. They have focused on gaining power, success, fame and wealth. The angels are helping us shift to an "advanced soul stage" where we *know we are spirit playing in a physical dimension*. The shift is shown by a concern broader than personal gain. The older soul will become aware that "We're all in this together." People are beginning to look at the planet and realize we have to take care of it or destroy ourselves. The focus is now more on peace within the globe, not just peace and comfort within one's self. People are beginning to reevaluate their concept of God and how their lives are affected by a Higher Power.

Who or What is God?

This chapter would not be complete without a discussion and a clarification of the image of God. The dictionary defines **god** (gŏd) *noun* in several ways:

"1. God. a. A being conceived as the perfect, omnipotent, omniscient originator and ruler of the universe, the principal object of faith and worship in monotheistic religions. b. The force, effect or a manifestation or aspect of this being. c. Christian Science. Infinite Mind; Spirit; Soul; Principle; Truth; Love (Mary Baker Eddy).

2. A being of supernatural powers or attributes, believed in and worshiped by a people, especially a male deity thought to control some part of nature or reality.

3. An image of a supernatural being; an idol.

4. One that is worshiped, idealized, or followed.

5. A very handsome man.

6. A powerful ruler or despot. [Middle English, from Old English.]"

There is so much controversy about concepts of "God" that wars have been fought over it. Each religion has its own belief as to who and what "God" is. There are an abundance of names given to this "Entity" or personification of "All That Is."

Hindus call God "Vedic" and follow Krishna as their prophet, believing in a "One God Who Is Many," and is called "Brahma, the World Soul, Cosmic Consciousness, Immortal Atman or Breath of Life, the Absolute, the Principle of Love and Law."

The Sanskrit writings have three basic truths: 1. The law of identification in which it is stated, "God and I are one," or "He who is yonder, yonder person, I am he." The soul is considered the only true self with all else illusion or *Maya*; 2. The law of *Karma* or the law of cause and effect; 3. The law of *Reincarnation* means "recurring life;" and says that what we sow we shall indeed reap if not in this life, then in another. While the Hindus believe in Reincarnation, the Christians believe in "Resurrection." I have wondered if they are speaking of the same thing. The Hindu believes that each person finds his representation of God from the level of his understanding, which changes with the accumulation of experiences in living. Their religion is very practical, never theoretical, subjective rather than objective. Of all religions, I can probably be in tune with Hinduism and Christianity.

Zoroastrianism is considered the oldest living religion in the world. . .if you consider religions with definite founders. It was said to be the foundation for Judaic and Christian religions. The Persian seer, Spitama Zoraster, lived six thousand years before Christ. In the Avesta, the sacred scripture of the Zoroastrians, it is stated the world was created in six days and a man named Mashya and a woman named Mashyoi were placed in a garden called Paradise, and then driven out because they disobeyed God. There are many other similarities to Christianity in their scriptures.

While the followers of Jesus Christ see God as the Trinity: Father (Power), Son (Love) and Holy Spirit (Action), the Zoroastrians believe in the Sacred Seven which represent aspects of God comparable to characteristics of people.

Buddhism, a religion of 150 million followers of which about 80 thousand are Americans, is built on the life of Gautama Buddha – a prince who became a beggar about 2,500 years ago. They believe this person came directly from heaven around 563 BC when Bodhisattva left his heavenly home to assume the form and nature of man. The doctrine made no distinction between race or the concept of caste. The sacred writings of Buddha were called Pitakas or baskets and contained "Ten Commandments:" 1. Thou shalt not kill. 2. Thou shalt not steal. 3. Thou shalt not commit adultery. 4. Thou shalt not be deceitful. 5. Thou shalt not curse. 6. Thou shalt not lie. 7. Thou shalt not speak vainly. 8. Thou shalt not covet. 9.

Thou shalt not insult or flatter. 10. Thou shalt be free from anger and revenge. This is very similar to the Christian Ten Commandments given by Moses.

Judaism as a faith goes back three thousand years and is recorded in the first five books of Moses, called the Pentateuch. It tells the saga of a people who guarded the Old Testament with their lives and, through centuries of persecution and tragic wars and death, believe they have now come into their own promised land – Israel. Jews firmly believe that God, Yahweh, chose Israel to be his people and Israel chose Yahweh to be their God. The Torah, their sacred scroll, is read every Sabbath, (Saturday), and means "law." It is the Jewish Bible and forms part of the Old Testament. While the Torah is written law, the Talmud was once oral law, but now has been brought together into the Mishnah and the Gemarah as rabbinical studies that interpret, illustrate and amplify written law.

The many Christian religions are based on the Bible which captured words of the master teacher, Jesus Christ. He is believed to be the Son of God and born of a virgin about 2,000 years ago. Many translate the Bible literally while others understand it figuratively, causing much controversy and many sects. Their belief in a "second coming" of Christ has caused many a doomsday prediction with only 144,000 to be saved. They believe that Christ rose from the dead and promised that all will also rise "on the last day."

Confucianism and Taoism are both ancient and modern religions. Confucius spoke truths 2,500 years ago that seem real today. Confucius spoke of governments consisting of choice officials to elevate ethical, just men in order to exert pressure upon crooked men, "for in this way the crooked may be made straight." Many of these familiar sayings are appropriate today.

Lao-tsu was a contemporary of Confucius. His name means "Old Philosopher." While Confucius taught how to live in the world, Lao-tsu helped people understand the world of spirit by following the Tao, or the Way of reason, the Way of life, and the Way of evolution. Both Confucius and Lao-tsu believed in keeping alive the truths of their ancestors and showing reverence to the old. These two giants are kept alive through the *Tao Te Ching*, (The book of the Way and of Virtue) and contains the essence of Taoism.

"There is no God but Allah! Come to prayer, come to prayer!" is the call of the Moslem crier in clear Arabic to come to Sabbath, observed on Friday. Followers of Mohammed pause in their work and face the Holy City of Mecca in Hejaz, Arabia, fold their hands, kneel and touch their foreheads to the ground. . .nearly 430 million of them. The people of Islam put emphasis on praying with the Koran as their scripture. This sacred text is learned from childhood on and is the center of their religion. It is believed the Koran is the inspired word of God given through Mohammed by the angel Gabriel and has never been revised or changed, unlike the Bible. Mohammed was born 570 years after Christ with the name Ubu'l Kassim and was influenced by the many religions of the Mecca. He was influenced by Jews he met on caravan trips to Palestine. He was intrigued by Christians whom he thought worshipped three gods – Father, Son and Holy Spirit. He also learned of Hindus who had one God, Brahma, as well as other religions of Asia. He found everyone had one thing in common: the need to find God.

Mohammedism began when Ubu'l Kassim envisioned the angel Gabriel who said, "Oh, Mohammed! Thou art Allah's messenger!" When the young man asked, "Who are you? Let me see your face!" the voice answered, "I am Gabriel. You are no longer Ubu'l Kassim. You are Mohammed, the prophet of Allah!" He was shown the words, "Read: In the name of Allah who created, who created man from a clot. Read: And thy lord is most bounteous who teacheth by the pen, teacheth man that which he knew not. Verily, man is rebellious. He thinketh himself independent. Lo, unto thy lord is the return!" That was how a religion was born.

Joseph Smith began the Mormon religion, (also called The Church of Latter Day Saints), because of a visit from an angel. It is one of many spin-offs from the Christian religion.

The Shinto religion originates in Japan but has no founder or prophet or Savior, no creed, scripture or theology. But it has churches, schools and priests. Shinto roots are set deep in mythology with a Shinto goddess called Amaterasu O-Mi-Kami – the

Heaven-Shining-Great. *Kami:* the power that creates, sustains, governs, and upholds everything in the universe and beyond. *Kami* is their name for God.

And, of course, I have a few names of my own. I call "It" "Pure Love," "Energy," "Pure Intelligence." Rather than the much abused and defiled word, "God," I prefer to use the Hindu word "Tao," (pronounced 'dow').

My concept of the Tao as It manifests in the physical is rather like the air we breath, swirling around and through everyone and everything. All we have to do is draw It into ourselves and be nourished by It. This Source of all Good answers to a multitude of names in a multitude of religions. I like to think of the Tao as the Source of all life – a powerful field of love-energy from which we draw the substance to create the physical dramas of our lives.

Joe has another way to picture this magnificent Energy. He imagines It like a huge generator that has to "download" Its powerful vibrations. It extends outward through bits of energy, like extension cords of Itself, that are plugged into angels who transmit that Energy to a lower frequency and plug It into ascended master teachers, such as Jesus, Mohammed or Buddha, who transmit that Energy to an even slower vibration and plug It into our souls. Because the Tao's Energy is so powerful, if we were to be in Its presence, we'd probably disintegrate – *poof!* We'd be dust. That may be where the "Fear of God" comes from. The Old Testament tells of people who were struck dead for simply touching the Arc of the Covenant!

But that really isn't the way the Tao works either, so we explore further – using an open mind and a playful imagination. Some say that we start as a spark from the Divine Flame and evolve through many lifetimes until we become pure Energy again and merge back into the Source. Until then, the Tao softens Its Power through mediators like angels. It assigns one to each of us so we have a direct link to the Source of all love, all knowledge, all goodness. But that isn't the whole picture either. To understand this Source of Power, we search through our concepts of energy.

Energy Fields

The angels explain that a soul dons a physical body and becomes human in order to learn how to manipulate energy in the physical world as part of gaining knowledge in the creative process. We are at the kindergarten level in the school of creating compared to our souls who are in high school and our angels who are in college. So we make mistakes. But it's all right. No one in the spirit world complains because they know we're just learning. Most of us humans are completely unaware that we're creating anything, let alone gaining expertise with it! And that expertise begins with an awareness of energy fields around each person or thing. Electromagnetic energy fields swirl around us, pulsating and changing with our thoughts and moods. Many psychics can see this as colors around the human body.

At my seminars, I take a coat hanger and make divining rods out of it. I place the handles in straws and show the participants how to measure their energy field. I hold the rods and stand about six feet from the person with the rods pointed slightly upward toward them. Then I move closer to the person until the rods cross. The straws prove I'm not manipulating the rods. I demonstrate this in the beginning of the seminar when the energy field is about two to three inches from the body, after the first meditation when it's about three feet from the body and at the end of the day's activities. Seeing the difference is awesome. Then I have a person demonstrate how a quartz crystal makes their aura, (energy field), flair out even wider. By the end of the seminar, we learn how to project the aura of Love across a room. It helps us understand that we can project our energy or thoughts even across a continent.

With all that has been covered in this book, not one word says as much as this demonstration of energy. It blows people away. Some can't wait to get home and test their friend's aura. I had a couple over after a seminar and the wife had to test her husband's aura. She was tickled to see it was very close to his body. It was almost like, "Ha, ha, I can do it better!" But it didn't take her husband long to figure out how to project love. At first he thought "sex" and we giggled when nothing happened. We figured out what he was thinking and told him that kind of "love" just won't do it...and it didn't. His aura withdrew! But when he really sent love, (it took a few minutes), the rods crossed 10 feet away! This demonstration helps us begin to understand the power of our thoughts and emotions. We begin to understand how we *do create our world.*

The Human Aura and Main Energy Centers

The word **chakra** is Sanskrit meaning a wheel and refers to the main energy centers in the human aura. C. W. Leadbeater describes them as "Wheel-like vortices which exist in the surface of the etheric double of man." The etheric is a description of a part of the spiritual body that clings to the physical body like the vessel of life-force.

Shirley MacLaine has written about her own inner transformation as she discovered what mystics have known for centuries – that we are spiritual beings within a physical body. She chuckles at the fears that some have about the "New Age" which she describes as ancient but new to the Western world. The Eastern religions have been kept from us for centuries by our own government.

The Supreme Court upheld legislative acts of Oriental Exclusion which not only kept out Asian immigrants, but most of their culture as well. It wasn't until 1943 with the influence of wartime Allies of Madame Chaing Kai Sheck and the Generalissimo that the law was changed. Isn't it amazing what fear can create? But we're waking up, thanks to the angels and the Tao.

According to many sources, chakras or main energy centers look like spinning lotus flowers. Their purpose and functions are summarized below:

Chakra One: Red; located at the spinal base; middle C frequency vibration; influences adrenal glands, kidneys and spinal column. It is where one experiences the "fight or flight" syndrome.

Chakra Two: Orange; located four fingers below the navel; D above middle C vibration; influences reproductive organs, governs creativity, attitudes in relationships and sex.

Chakra Three: Yellow; solar plexus; E above Middle C vibration; influences pancreas, liver, spleen, stomach, gall bladder and aspects of the nervous system. It is a clearinghouse for emotional sensitivities and issues of personal power.

Chakra Four: Green; heart; F above middle C vibration; influences thymus gland, heart, blood and circulatory system, and immune and endocrine systems. Center through which we feel love.

Chakra Five: Blue; throat; G above middle C vibration; influences thyroid gland, lungs, vocal cords, bronchial apparatus, metabolism. Center of expression, communication, judgment.

Chakra Six: Indigo; center of forehead (Third Eye); A above Middle C vibration, 440 vibrations per second; influences pituitary gland, lower brain and nervous system, ears, nose and left eye (eye of personality) and how we consider our spiritual nature.

Chakra Seven: Violet; top of head; B above middle C vibration; influences pineal gland, upper brain and right eye. Our connection with the Tao.

It would make sense that these energy centers are the main trunk line for the life flow. If we get out of balance, we block energy and create pain or illness. When we notice something within the body that isn't right, we can increase energy by simply humming the vibration that aligns us with that chakra. This is where chanting in ancient times makes sense. They knew how to bring the body, mind, emotions and soul back together when it was out of whack. Don't laugh when you hear someone sounding, "Ommm..." Perhaps you should join them!

Edgar Cayce told of an incident where he was about to step into an elevator in a hotel. The door opened, but he froze on the spot. The door closed and the elevator crashed to the bottom, killing all who were in it. Cayce did not enter the elevator because he realized later that *no one had an aura*. Their "lights" or electromagnetic fields were gone. This was moments before their deaths. Could the spirit or soul have left the body, knowing it was about to leave it for good? I believe this occurs in many cases. Cayce reacted in the moment and his life was spared.

There are new techniques in photography to actually show the human aura in all its remarkable colors. It is interesting to see how colors change with moods and feelings of the individual.

I see auras with the help of my angels. An impression of color is given to me through my mind's eye and I become aware of the meaning that goes with it. Just as the individual's angel may sometimes show itself to me in a specific color to signify a message, so too, does the imaging of the aura. When I see a lot of grey in the aura, I know the person's life energy is very low. When I see red sparks shooting out from the body, I know that area is unhealthy. But when I see a rainbow of colors surrounding the person, I know I'm with an old soul and my spirit rejoices.

If you think of the play on words we have developed in our language about colors, you can begin to understand how the aura has influenced most of us even when we can't see it. For example, to "see red" means to be very angry. We wave a red cloth before a bull to make him charge. We picture kings in royal garments of red velvet, signifying leadership. We imagine orange as an energy boost because of its vibrancy, yet we consider yellow a cowardly color. It must be a mustard yellow, not the golden sun-yellow of the chakra of creativity. We think of green as growth and healing and pink as love. Colors are vibrations that can be healing or destructive.

Feng Shui

Color is an important factor in the ancient Chinese study of energy called "Feng Shui" (pronounced fung shway). One man had a fast-growing cancer that doctors said would kill him within months. He called in the Feng Shui doctors and asked if perhaps his home was the cause of his illness. They entered a home that was all green: walls, carpet and furniture. Green symbolizes growth. This man had growths within his body. The "House Doctors" immediately moved the man out and set to work changing the walls to other pastel colors and rearranging the furniture and pictures to create what is called "Good Ch'I" (pronounced chee), and what I call "energy." A year later, the man was still alive and very well.

Feng Shui is a concept that is about four or five thousand years old. For example, many people are aware of the Asian symbol of Yin and Yang as the negative and positive principles of universal life like the Pendulum of Opposites in Chapter Three. During celebrations of Christmas, or Hanukkah, or someone's birthday, we all light candles, representing good energy. The red color of Christmas is also a color that brings increased financial energy. There are many more things you can add to your home to bring it healthy energy that will flow within your body and help to increase healing and well-being.

Good Feng Shui

Living Things: Plants represent life and growth, circulating energy and opportunity; plants in an office boost productivity; live or silk flowers are a great energy boost.

Colors: Black and red symbolize wealth and happiness. Brown and tan give focus and grounding. Yellow and gold represent intellect and prosperity. Green symbolizes growth, new opportunity. Purple and light blues express tranquility and spiritual awareness.

Bright Objects: Mirrors, reflective metallic items, crystals, prisms and shiny coins.

Harmonious Sound: Wind chimes, music boxes, musical instruments (even pictures are beneficial), stereos.

Moving Objects: Fish tanks with bubbling water, windsocks, mobiles, water fountains.

Bad Feng Shui

Dead Things: Dried or plastic flowers, animal skins or heads, pictures of dead people.

Colors: Patterns that are too busy, animal skins, overemphasis on one color, contrasts that are too sharp and distinct.

Dark Objects or Places: Basements, cluttered closets, drawers, darkened rooms.

Clashing Sounds: Arguing, hammering, sawing, buzzing neon lights, high power lines nearby.

Dead Spaces: Places where energy can be trapped, such as spiral staircases, which are sometimes called "corkscrews to hell."

Lines: Vertical lines like striped wallpaper or overhead beams; square or rectangle pictures lined up on a wall. Energy needs to flow with curved lines and round tables or oval frames.

The study of your home and the areas surrounding it can be fascinating from the viewpoint of Feng Shui. To assess the ch'i power spots in your home, take compass in hand, minus wrist watch and bracelets, begin at the front door and move through every room of your house to determine true north, south, etc. For example, if you place your favorite chair in the northwest corner of your living room, you'll create more recreation time. If your kitchen is in the eastern section of the house, you'll promote healthier eating habits. When I learned to put something red in the southeast corner of my home to promote incoming money, I remembered how I had listened to my angels the year before to put my hooked Santa on my jewelry cabinet in the southeast corner of the bedroom. Joe loves to buy me jewelry on my birthday, our anniversary and at Christmas. Is it coincidence that my readings have increased, my lecture series has taken off and my book is about to be published as I write this? Although retired, Joe has increased his income through code enforcement that reflects a growing economy in our area.

I told my friend, Susan, about the red in the southeast corner. She looked around her living room, located the right spot and exclaimed, "I've got my grandma's red lamp there! No wonder I have a waiting list for my crafts. Maybe that's why my husband's business has doubled." We both stared at one another in amazement. Fact or fiction? If Susan was negative, complaining and whining, I doubt it would be the same. She is a kindred spirit in her upbeat energy and positive outlook on life.

The following enables you to do a quick survey of your home to increase needed good energy in particular power spots:

House Power Spots	Meaning
North	Career and Work
Northeast	Learning and Skill
East	Health and Family
Southeast	Finance and Wealth
South	Peer Acknowledgment
Southwest	Love and Relationships
West	Children and Pets
Northwest	Travel and Assistance

Remember, if you want to promote any of these areas, place some of the "good ch'i" in that particular spot like candles, crystals, plants or flowers, etc. One young couple wanted children, but had had no luck. They placed figurines of children on the west side of their home. Within a short time, they had a child.

Acupuncture: Opening Energy Centers

Acupuncture is an ancient technique of using needles placed in the center of energy vortexes of the human body to open the flow of energy. Many have received relief from pain and have found healing through this therapy. Acupressure is a form of acupuncture that also works quite well. There are many books which show "trigger points" where energy can be blocked and thus create pain. By gentle pressure at these points, pain stops and the flow of energy reopens.

I traveled with Joe and another couple many miles for them to receive acupuncture treatments to stop smoking. I didn't want to be left out, so I asked if something could be done to help my tendency toward chronic bronchitis. Sure enough, I found myself on a table with little needles sticking out of my chest, legs and feet. The doctor stated three things that set me up for bronchitis: sweets, caffeine and dairy products. When she tried to find the place inside my knees to put needles that referred to my "sweet center," she asked which part was the most tender. "All of it!" I exclaimed. She said that after the treatment, I wouldn't crave sweets. She was right! It was six months before I indulged in sweets again and messed up what I had gained, like an alcoholic who'd fallen off the wagon.

Acupuncture worked for the other couple who haven't smoked in five years, but for Joe it lasted 10 weeks before he was pacing the floor in the basement, counting the cinder blocks! They said that of all the addictions, smoking was the most difficult to break.

Healing Through Energy

There are people who have learned to manipulate the energy surrounding the human body for healing. With the help of their angelic guides, they intuitively sense what is wrong with a patient even before a doctor has diagnosed them. We've already spoken of the great psychic of the forties, Edgar Cayce, whose work is well-documented. Ruth Montgomery tells of a "Mr. A." who also could manipulate energy by drawing it into his own body and then send it to a patient. Dr. Caroline Myss has been working with her form of "energy medicine" for some time. Dr. Bernie Siegel has helped people cure themselves from cancer and other related illnesses. Dr. Deepak Chopra is also a well-known doctor who teaches people about energy and healing of body, mind and soul. The angels are awakening all of us to begin to become aware of energy on many levels so that we, too, can become healers for ourselves and others.

Near-Dear Experiences

Dr. Raymond Moody stumbled on to his first "near-death experience" as he tried to resuscitate a person whom he had to declare lost. He had already written the death certificate when the patient returned and told of his incredible experience. That changed the doctor's career direction to focus on near-death experiences. In his studies, he found that almost everyone related an extraordinary sequence of events that occurred: floating above the body, seeing doctors trying to revive them, seeing loved ones grieving; going through a tunnel; meeting a being of light at the end where other deceased loved ones also greeted them; and seeing a panoramic life review. Some were given a choice whether to stay or return. When they choose to return, their lives are changed for the better and *they never fear death again.*

One interesting account is told by Dr. George Ritchie, a respected doctor who was about to be released from the service because he had been accepted into medical school. He was very excited about the prospect. But he contacted pneumonia and "died." He recalls his panic that he had to get to medical school and found himself traveling along a darkened street where he paused to ask directions. No one seemed to respond. Again, he tried to speak to people and found someone who could answer – another spirit! The doctor nearly panicked when he realized he was dead. He had to go to medical school! He had to get back into his own body. He suddenly found himself back in the hospital. He couldn't recognize his body until he spotted his ring on his hand dangling from a gurney covered with a sheet. He immediately willed himself back into the body and chuckles as he remembers the startled orderly who saw his sheet move. His account of the out-of-body travel was verified when he did make that trip to medical school. He told the people in the car what to expect in the next town where none of them had been before. . .in the body, that is.

Betty Eadie describes the "tunnel" as "deep rumbling, rushing sound. . .a movement that seemed unrelenting. But although the sound and power were awesome, I was filled again with a very pleasant feeling – almost hypnotic. Darkness began to surround my being. I was gently drawn up into a great, whirling, black mass."

My angels have explained the tunnel as an energy vortex in which vibrations of the individual are raised and adjusted to be able to exist in the higher frequency dimension of spirit. I've found no written documents that back this up, but then it took some time for me to read the many books I've mentioned. Perhaps I'll run across one that verifies this as well.

Eadie goes on to speak of "the light at the end of the tunnel" – (I wonder where that saying came from) – and describes it as the most unconditional love she has ever felt. I know it seems unbelievable that this is the love I feel when I give a reading in which angels are present. I find it quite awesome myself. But when most psychics complain of drained energy after many readings, I feel increased energy and a sense of great joy. My body may feel tired, but after all, I *am* over sixty! The energy can sometimes keep me up at night if I've given readings late. I've found that obsidian, a lovely black rock that is actually volcanic lava, can ground me and bring me back to Earth. Yet, some say obsidian is beneficial in improving the higher vision of spiritual awareness. We could do a whole chapter on the healing powers of crystals alone.

Out-of Body Projection or Astral Travel

When one has had an "out-of-body" experience, they become

a believer. . .if they aren't too frightened to ever want to try it again. My younger brother, who was also psychic, was able to astral travel at will. He tells of the time he and mom were on a trolley going downtown Detroit when he suddenly was back home, observing our aunt and uncle arriving. He was about five at the time. He tried to get mom to go back home, but she, of course, didn't pay any attention. He told her they had left a basket of apples. Sure enough, when they got home, there were the apples with a note. Yet Jim, (not his real name), learned not to share his experiences with others after that.

Since I was raised by that aunt and uncle, I didn't grow up with Jim. It wasn't until in our late fifties that he revealed to me his extraordinary abilities. He had heard that I was "into reincarnation" at a Thanksgiving family gathering where we began to share our experiences. Each of us had kept it secret because of family pressures and beliefs. What a joy it was to be able to talk with him, to exchange ideas, to learn together. But we lived so far apart and soon he was on the other side in the world of spirit. I miss him. I know his family misses him even more.

But What About the Next World?
The Transition Of Death

When we lose a loved one, we go through a grieving process of letting go. It doesn't happen overnight. One of my students lost her father from a brain tumor. We discussed how his long illness gave the family an opportunity to let go. They had time to say good-bye. I remember my own two brothers' experiences of cancer. It was a blessing to have time to visit and remember good times before they were gone from our sight, but not our hearts.

It seems all we have left are memories. We tend to remember good times and forget the bad. We tend to hang on to that memory and the pain of loss continues to gnaw away at our heart, leaving a hole that can't seem to be filled. Time shifts backwards and traps us. When we come to understand that a loved one has not "passed away," but rather has become its true self again – spirit – we can release it to go on to its own continued life's purpose. It can come and go with the wind. It can stand beside you and comfort you, touch you and speak to you. When you let go of the pain and become aware of their peace and joy, you can communicate with them. They are not gone. They are still here.

Jackie and her brothers and sisters were with her father when he took his last breath. She stood at the foot of the bed, watching all the others gathered around. She began to see their energy fields and was in awe of it. When she focused on her father, she couldn't see his energy, but as she looked up, she saw it separated from his body, hovering above. She exclaimed out loud, "Oh, there you are!" The family turned in unison and looked at her. She shrugged and said, "Oh, nothing." As she looked again at her father, she noticed that he was still breathing, but within moments, he had taken his last breath. The experience moved her greatly, but she was only able to share it with very few people. What a shame!

Yet, it is not good to try to hold on to those who die, demanding they stay by you. One mother lost her son to AIDS. Her heart was broken. When she came for a reading, her son came through and tried to comfort his mother. He let her know he had chosen that life to gain balance between previous lifetimes of being too "macho." As a gay man, he learned how men can be gentle, kind, nurturing and loving – and still be male.

He begged his mother to let him get on with his life. For in the next dimension, he had many exciting things to do. He told how some spirits continue on with their studies, while others act as rescue teams to greet spirits who have died a sudden death. He commented how good it was that he had a prolonged dying because he could prepare his family for the loss. His mother cried copiously, but try as she may, she could not let go of him. . .yet. When a loved one dies, we miss them, but we must let them go into their future. It is not kind to hold them back.

Death is truly a given – a fact of life you can count on. It will be so for each one of us. For those who fear death, it can be quite traumatic. For those who have no fear of the next world, their passing is easy and comfortable. They are greeted by their angel and escorted to the "land of milk and honey" where they rest for awhile and then review their life.

One delightful movie on this subject is *Defending Your Life*, the story of a young man who purchases a brand new Mercedes and promptly crashes into a bus and dies. His adventures in the astral plane are not too far off from my studies of the afterlife. For example, in a restaurant, he orders a simple breakfast that is immediately given to him. He is sure there has been some mistake and that he must have been given someone else's order. "No, it's no mistake. Anything you can think of in this place is immediately created." He also discovers you are never full or fat! When Joe saw this movie, he was ready to die. He loves food.

In this movie, Shirley MacLaine acts as the hawker to the "Past Life Pavilion." The essence of the story is to determine how this man had lived his life – in fear or in love, a great lesson for all of us.

People are learning to accept death as a natural part of life. It is heartening to know that an organization like Hospice has sprung up to meet the needs of the dying. Both patient and caregiver profit from this experience through knowledge about life after death.

So many people assume that once we "pass over" we gain immediate knowledge and wisdom and know all things. That's simply not true. Whatever knowledge we leave this life with, we keep. After a long rest in the astral plane, we can go on to gain more knowledge, but we still do not know all that is. Only God does. And each time we return, we agree to forget all that we know to play the game again. But if we're open to our soul and angel, they'll let memories slip through as we mature.

My "Halo Club" studied the book, *A Soul's Journey,* by Peter Richelieu, (Thorsons, 1996). It is about a young man who grieves over the death of his brother. In July, 1941, he learns his brother, only twenty-three, has been killed in action in England. He is bitter against the "Powers that Be, the beneficent Creator who is talked of so glibly. How could He be beneficent if He allowed the innocent to be killed?" Being raised a Christian, he admits that he took many things for granted, until an eastern Indian appears at his door and claims that Peter has sent for him. Although denying this, the man insists he has indeed called him. The whole book details, in diary form, Peter's out-of-body experiences to the seven levels of the astral world. In the first level, he meets his brother who is extremely happy, enjoying life in a world exactly like London. He frequents his favorite pubs and even dates beautiful women. In other planes, people are pursuing intellectual knowledge, studying musical instruments, performing scientific experiments. In still other planes, he finds beautiful countryside homes with gardens. In each one, they seem to reflect the Christian belief that he also holds.

"On the other side," Richelieu's guide, Acharya, explains, "we see the full and complete results of all our actions: few of us do not suffer in the seeing and register a vow that in future lives we shall act differently." According to this wise guide, Peter is shown how we pass through lower astral levels into higher ones as we gain knowledge and mature.

The questions of "heaven" and "hell" were discussed as well, stating what my angels had previously revealed: whatever our belief system dictates while we're alive will be created in the astral world when we die. If we believe we deserve a hell, then we will create one. . .until it no longer serves us and then we move to the "Light" and continue to learn and grow. But most people do not believe they deserve a hell and consequently create a beautiful "heaven."

There were several particularly interesting questions at the end of the book. One discussed the idea of race, asking if one race was more evolved than another. Peter's guide replied, "From a spiritual point of view there is no reason to suppose that a white skin is necessarily better than a colored skin. . .[and] does not denote his standing in evolution." He goes on to say the nation into which a person will be born is decided by more evolved souls as to the characteristics he may choose to gain or overcome, stating, "It is certainly not chance which decides whether a man is born an Englishman, an American, a German or a Chinese."

Since I often see animals in spirit, I wondered about their "evolution" as well. I remember one reading in particular where I saw a little white dog in spirit begging for my attention. When I mentioned it to my client, she said that she did have a little poodle named Cookie. I told her it was telling us to go to another room where there was a desk and to look in the top, right-hand drawer where there was a picture of a dog. Since I had never been in this person's home before, I was not aware of a room with a desk, nor anything about her dog. We both went to the room and found a drawing she had done of Snoopy. I found out that she did birthday cards for people with funny Snoopy cartoons on it. Her dog, Cookie, let it be known to me that she was to put aside Snoopy and instead write "Cookie Says" cards. It was from the well-known saying, "Confucius Says. . ." that my client created her successful "Cookie Says. . ." cards. This lady followed her dog's advice and now has many of her cards in shops.

Animals do go to the astral plane but for a shorter period than we do before they join their "group" soul and take on another animal body. When I first heard the concept of "group souls," I was confused. Richelieu's book explains it to my satisfaction. When a spirit decides to explore the physical world, it does it thoroughly. First it merges with various aspects of the mineral kingdom, through the plant kingdom, into the animal kingdom – first the wild animals, then domesticated, and then pets with humans. It does not *become* the animal, but rather merges *with* the personality of the animal, experiencing physical life through it. When the soul has had a close relationship with a human and has lost all fear of people, it is ready to create a physical body and begin the entire cycle of human incarnations. Then it truly *becomes* the individual for that particular lifetime.

Well, if you haven't thrown this book out the window by now, there's more about those many lives you have been through and are still ahead of you. So many people I've seen almost panic when they believe they may have to live another "hard" life. I know I did. But now I understand it's simply not possible for a person to learn all it needs or wants to learn in one lifetime. And we keep on learning during the lives in-between at various astral levels.

The Michael teachings were so clearly truth to me that I was instantly accepting of the majority of them. No one can completely accept everything that is in print. There's too many contradictory concepts. But once in awhile, something touches your heart and it sings, "YES!" The Michael concept of soul evolution made great sense to me. The more I studied it, the more it rang true. Below is a bare-bones summary of these teachings:

Cycles of the Soul

The following is a summary from *The Michael Handbook* by Dr. Jose Stevens and Simon Warwick-Smith:

Infant: Often psychic; attuned to nature rather than people; simple, childlike, lives in the moment; focus is on the body and how to use and operate it; guarded, has much fear; tests society's rules for limits; lives on the edge of society; often isolated; sex is animalistic; sly; clever; no personal relationships; creates massive amounts of karma; no conscience; society often locks them up. Two examples are the well-known case of a child raised by wolves and the Unabomber incident.

Baby: Starts to care what other people think of them to the point of obsession to obtain love and admiration from another; solid member of society; good citizen; loyal, family-oriented; looks to authority to do the right thing; belongs to a traditional religion; joins clubs, etc.; can display bizarre behavior; very rigid, unbending and dogmatic in beliefs; operates more from emotions rather than reason and can be brutal and violent; begins to show authority over others as power play; still very fear-driven; little conscience. Colonel Kaddafy of Libya is an example of a baby soul.

Young: Expresses anger as cover for fears; can be domineering, dogmatic; uses "rules" of religion and society as authority; doesn't like people much; great fear of criticism; can be very set in their ways; authoritative; uses wealth and power to control others; wants to do what's popular; very status-conscious; wants to be right, famous and successful; feels something lacking and can't identify it; still not too much conscience. Jim and Tammy Baker, Mao Tsetung, Ferdinand and Imelda Marcos are examples of young souls.

Mature: Starts to recognize the importance of emotional attachment, but buries it at first, causing inner conflict between success and relationship; not too materially successful; agonizes over relationships and issues that become more important than anything, such as finding a soul mate or saving the environment; great emotional drama; likes to express personality through dress; finds themselves in a soap-opera life; very attached to people. Marilyn Monroe, Marlon Brando, William Shakespeare; Ernest Hemingway, Mozart and Richard Burton are examples.

Old: Gaining in confidence; hovers between drama and objectivity, causing internal warfare; quiet and goes within to seek knowledge; takes on a very laid-back almost eccentric attitude; kindly; spiritual with focus on teaching; authoritative with power; extremely busy; hard working; spirituality very important; doesn't rest often; trust issues; only "self" karma left such as finding self worth; can tend to be lazy. At the end of the cycle, the soul becomes introverted, teaching one or two people and has only acceptance issues left. Carl Jung, James Joyce, Walt Whitman, Abraham Lincoln and George Burns are examples.

Transcendental: No longer needs a physical body; has the ability to see beyond the personality and the illusion of physical plane. Previously very few appeared, but now many are appearing because of the shift from a majority of young souls to a majority of mature souls on the planet. Mahatma Gandhi is an example.

Infinite: Representation of the Tao (God) and comes to Earth every two thousand years with a worldwide impact for literally thousands of years. There are often magical and mystical events surrounding the birth of these exalted beings and their presence is felt and prophesied long before their arrival. Jesus Christ, Buddha, Lao Tsu and Ra are examples of the infinite soul.

Summary

Life is a wonderful gift. If nothing else, we can begin to imagine the vast universe the Tao has created and have respect for our minuscule part within it. Yet, we are all One with All That Is, making each part as important as the whole. So often we tend to belittle ourselves through comparisons with others. We are uniquely designed and made by our souls with the help of guides, our angels and the Tao. The design of our bodies, minds, emotions and personalities has been created to serve a divine purpose for the life we have been so blessed to receive. Make no mistake about it. There is a divine plan for you, and you are living it perfectly right now. Bless it and rejoice in it.

Journal Entries for Week Eight

Directions: Answer the questions below in your journal. Take time to meditate on your answers; they reveal deep-seated beliefs that are the basis to understanding your actions and reactions to life.

1. Practice taking a deep breath, counting backward from three to one and entering your Inner Sanctum. Visualize your angel leading you into deeper and deeper meditation.
2. Define God. How does He/She/It figure in your life?
3. Do you worship God in a religious setting? If yes, describe the rituals, doctrines and scriptures that form the basis of your beliefs. If no, what are the beliefs governing your actions?
4. Using the "Cycle of Souls," where is your soul on this evolutionary cycle? Where are your family members and friends?

5. Describe the beliefs of your partner or loved ones.
6. How are these beliefs compatible or incompatible with your own? How do you compromise when there are differences?
7. Do you belong to any support group that meets on a regular basis? If not, would you like to? If so, what qualities and objectives would you like it to have?
8. What form of prayer do you use regularly? Do you pray on a regular basis? Do you meditate daily?
9. What would you say now is the Divine Plan for your life? How have you been uniquely created and prepared for this?

Selected Bibliography and Recommended Reading

Allen, James. *As A Man Thinketh.* CA: Devorss Publ.

Altea, Rosemary. *The Eagle and the Rose.* NY: Warner Books, 1995.

American Heritage Dictionary of the English Language, Third Edition. Houghton Mifflin Co., 1995.

Angel Decoder. Australia: Dynamo House Pty. Ltd.

Bach, Marcus. *Major Religions of the World.* CA: DeVorss & Co., 1959.

Benedictine Monks of Santo Domingo de Silos. *Chant.* Spain: Original sound recording by HISPAVOX, 1982.

Bunker, Dusty. *Dream Cycles.* MA: Para Research, Inc., 1981.

Chopra, Deepak. *Ageless Body, Timeless Mind: The Quantum Alternative to Growing Old.* NY: Harmony Books, 1993.

A Course In Miracles, Three-volume set. CA: Foundation for Inner Peace, 1992.

Davidson, Gustav. *A Dictionary of Angels Including the Fallen Angels.* NY: The Free Press, 1971.

Dixon, Jeane. *My Life and Prophecies.* NY: William Morrow & Co., 1970.

Eadie, Betty J. *Embraced By The Light.* CA: Gold Leaf Press, 1992.

Fairchild, Dennis. *Healing Homes Feng Shui Here & Now.* MI: Wavefield Books, 1996.

Faraday, Ann, Ph.D. *Dream Power.* NY: Berkley Publ. Corp., 1972.

Faraday, Ann, Ph.D. *The Dream Game.* NY: Harper & Row, Pub., 1974.

Gawain, Shakti. *Living in the Light.* CA: New World Library, 1986.

Gawain, Shakti. *Reflections in the Light,* comp. Denise Grimshaw. CA: New World Library, 1988.

Grubb, Nancy and Mary Christian, eds. *Angels in Art.* NY: Abbeville, 1995.

Hay, Louise. *You Can Heal Your Life.* CA: Hay House, 1987.

Hill, Napoleon. *Think and Grow Rich.* CA: Melvin Powers Wilshire Co., 1966.

Kreeft, Peter. *Angels (and Demons).* CA: Ignatius Press, 1995.

Leadbeater, C.W. *The Chakras.* IL: Theosophical Pub. House, 1972. Page 1.

Lerner, Isha and Mark. *Inner Child Cards: A Journey Into Fairy Tales, Myth, and Nature.* NM: Bear & Co., 1992.

March, Marion and Joan McEvers. *The Only Way to Learn Astrology, Volume 1.* CA: ACS Pub., 1981, 5521 Ruffin Rd., San Diego, CA 92123, (619) 492–9919.

Moody, Raymond, Jr., M.D. *Life After Life.* NY: Bantam, 1975.

Myss, Carolyn, Ph.D. *Anatomy of the Spirit.* NY: Harmony Books, 1996.

Newton, Michael, Ph.D. *Journey of Souls.* MN: Llewellyn Pub., 1995.

Pattent, Arnold. *You Can Have It All.* OR: Beyond Worlds Pub., 1995.

Ponder, Catherine. *The Dynamic Laws of Prosperity.* NJ: Prentice Hall, 1962.

Price, Hope. *Angels: True Stories of How They Touch Our Lives.* NY: Avon Books, 1993.

Price, John Randolph. *The Abundance Book.* TX: Quartus Books, 1987.

Prudden, Bonnie. *Pain Erasure The Bonnie Prudden Way.* NY: Ballantine Books, 1980.

Pruitt, James. *The Complete Angel.* NY: Avon Books.

Ramer, Andrew. *Angel Answers.* NY: Pocket Books, 1995.

Redfield, James. *The Celestine Prophecy.* NY: Warner Books, 1993.

Richelieu, Peter. *A Soul's Journey.* CA: HarperCollins Publ., 1958.

Roberts, Jane. *The Coming of Seth.* NY: Pocket Book, 1976.

Rodegast, Pat and Judith Stanton, comp. *Emmanuel's Book; Emmanuel's Book II: A Choice for Love; Emmanuel's Book III: What is an Angel Doing Here?* NY: Bantam Books, 1987; 1989; 1994.

Scott, Cyril, ed. *The Boy Who Saw True.* Essex: C.W. Daniel Co., 1961.

Stern, Jess. *Edgar Cayce, The Sleeping Prophet.* NY: Bantam Books, 1968.

Stevens, Jose Luis and Simon Warwick-Smith. *The Michael Handbook.* CA: Warwick Press, 1988.

Sullivan, Betty Brisse (Calleja). *Let's Make Music.* NJ: Jam Handy and Prentice Hall, 1972.

Sullivan, Betty Brisse (Calleja). *Exciting Language Arts Projects.* ME: J. Weston Walsh, Publ., 1984.

Taylor, Terry Lynn. *Messengers of Light.* CA: J.H. Kramer Inc., 1990. Page 94.

Warter, Carlos, M.D., Ph.D. *Recovery of the Sacred: Lessons in Soul Awareness.* FL: Health Communications, Inc., 1994.

Weed, Joseph J. *Wisdom of the Mystic Masters.* NY: Parker Publ., 1968.

About the Author

Betty Rae Calleja has a Master's Degree in Education with over 40 years of teaching experience. She is a published author, composer, artist, lecturer, psychic and visionary. Betty Rae has hundreds of clients across the United States, from Texas to California to New York to Florida. Betty Rae and her husband, Joe, are completing an addition to their home on fifteen wooded acres in Otter Lake, Michigan. "Angel House" will be open in early 1998 for weekend retreats, seminars and workshops to all angel lovers. She welcomes any questions or comments.

Betty Rae Calleja can be reached at:
6140 White Sand Drive
Otter Lake, Michigan 48464